Leaning Forward

Surviving and Winning
In the Future of Interactive Marketing

by
Josh Linkner

First published by Dog Ear Publishing
4010 W. 86th Street, Ste H
Indianapolis, IN 46268
www.dogearpublishing.net

dog Near
PUBLISHING

ISBN: 978-159858-428-8

This book is printed on acid-free paper.

Printed in the United States of America

Dedication:

To my amazing, funny, spirited, and crazy family – Dana, Noah, and Chloe.

Acknowledgements:

I want to thank so many people for their help and contribution in making this book a reality. Special thanks to Eli Greenbaum for his exquisite penmanship, research, and thoughtfulness. Thanks to Alesya Opelt, one of the best marketers I've met. Thanks to dozens of dedicated ePrize team members for their help and insight including: Jordan Broad, Robb Lippitt, Drew Bennett, Ivan Frank, Matt Kates, Robyn Marcotte, Tia Kouchary, Bob Marsh, Gerry Miller, Neil Rosenzweig, Allison Doyle, Kaiser Yang, Josh Glantz, Jackie Trepanier, Gary Shuman, Gabe Karp, and Nathan Hughes. Special thanks to Dan Gilbert, Brian Hermelin, David Katzman, and Gary Shiffman for their support, friendship, and mentorship. Thanks to all those who helped change an industry, and had the courage to try new things. Finally, special thanks to my family: Jack and Judy Rosenzweig, Robert and Renita Linkner, Monica Farris Linkner, Mickey Farris, and Dana, Noah, and Chloe Linkner. Thank you for your unwavering love and support. This would not be possible without you.

Table of Contents

INTRODUCTION

This book is obsolete.

This book is obsolete.

And it's important.

Important enough that it could make all the difference in your success – or failure – as a marketer, as a brand advertiser, as a businessperson, as an entrepreneur in the world of interactive promotional marketing.

This book is obsolete in the same way your state-of-the-art computer was obsolete the minute you bought it. As was the audio system you listen to. And the car you drive. They were out-of-date the minute you bought them because everything is always moving ahead and there's always something new out there. That's just the way it is. But they are still important because they lay the groundwork for what's coming down the pipeline.

The same is true in marketing.

Because there, too, everything is changing so fast (thank you, technology), and if you aren't on top of it, you're out of it.

And if you're out of it, you haven't got a prayer in competing for your share of the market place, your share of the consumer's mind, or, most important, your share of the consumer's wallet.

Chances are when you bought your first computer light years ago, you studied the industry, shopped around, talked to geek friends, read reviews, compared prices, options, upgrades and finally made your purchase. Or maybe you were one of those people who took the recommendation of a salesperson and bought what was available that day that moment. In either case, you probably found out soon afterwards that someone somewhere was introducing an updated chip or bigger memory or enhanced speakers or faster CD burner or something that said, "Sorry, pal. Your state-of-the-art desktop computer is ancient history." Yesterday was yesterday. And yesterday's gone. But that first computer was valuable and up-to-the-minute when you got it and it gave you the knowledge and insight to understand and appreciate the newer, better computers you've had since then. That's what we'll do here with the New World of Marketing.

This book is intended to help you understand what has happened in interactive promotional marketing, where we believe it is going, why it's important and to arm you with the insight we've gained at ePrize. All that so you know how to tackle interactive marketing in the future so that you not only survive, but that you succeed. Otherwise, there's every possibility you will fail.

It is our obligation to point out that the interactive promotional marketing field is dynamic. As interactive marketing shifts into new and dramatic forms often nuanced as "permission-based" or "action marketing," we know that its structure and shape will continuously change with the development of new technology and a better understanding of the ever-more sophisticated consumer we address.

It's all changing even as we speak and you read. But what you read here will serve as a roadmap to the future as interactive marketing evolves hand-in-hand with technology and the marketing imagination.

Just in case you're wondering, we know of what we speak. At ePrize, we've created and executed literally thousands of successful online promotions – including interactive sweepstakes, points-based rewards programs and chance-to-win promotions – across all industries. Our experience with interactive marketing has been successful not just for us, but also for our clients: companies that populate the Fortune 500 and whose brands are part of a global economy and vocabulary; companies such as Coca-Cola, Proctor & Gamble, Dell, General Mills, Honda, Citibank, Yahoo, Duracell and plenty of others. We've been able to help them carve out, expand and solidify their market shares. And we've done it through the growing phenomena of promotional marketing, or, let's be even more specific, *interactive* promotional marketing, a form of marketing that delivers predictable, measurable results and didn't really come into its own until the advent of the Digital Revolution – a revolution that changed the playing field (it didn't level it; on the contrary, it transformed it entirely and tipped it in favor of those who knew what was going on).

If you insist on doing things the way you did 20, 10, five years or even a year ago, look out behind you. Pre-Digital Revolution marketing thinking will hurt you. You will be trampled upon and putting up an "Out of Business" sign on your door before you realize it. It boils down to adapt or die. Darwinism at its finest.

Much of that has to do with a changing population that is very much at home with the new technologies – a generation that has grown up during or after the Digital Revolution, a generation that has never known life without a laptop, cell phone, Sony Playstation, ATMs and has always thought of "downloading" as a natural act.

We all remember the jokes that were made when VCRs were introduced. The 35-year-old dad would buy it, but it was the nine-year-old kid that would program it. That is what's happening now. The generation that's coming, and come, into its own, the generation that will soon be running the world, has grown up with technologies that often baffle previous generations. An uncomfortable realization? Perhaps. But if you're in charge of a major television network, a major advertising agency, a Fortune 500 company, or even a "mom 'n' pop" dry cleaners, then you know you have to address not just what's here now, but also what's on the horizon. That means looking at new methods of communication to identify and address your target markets. Consequently, rethinking the allocation of your marketing budget and reassessing the most effective ways to connect with that generation because they – along with current and coming generations – are the ones you'll be selling to in the future. How will you engage them?

As a traditional marketer, how much longer can you rely on – and place your advertising dollars into – commercials on television programs watched by a shrinking audience; into print ads in newspapers with consistently lower circulation numbers? Sure, those commercials and ads can be entertaining, amusing, even appealing, but do they translate into results?

How do you know?

When will you realize that a Web site is not significantly different from those traditional forms of advertising unless it is alive and compelling and interactive? When will you take the steps that will change the nature of your marketing efforts from forcefully intruding into the consumer's life and instead being invited, even welcomed, into the consumer's mind?

You can do all that. Maybe you already are. If not, you should – you better.

You *want* those consumers to be engaged, to hear, see and understand your message. You want them to *lean forward*, to build a one-on-one relationship with them. You can't do that efficiently any longer through traditional mass marketing. But you can through effective, relevant and visible promotional efforts. And the Digital Revolution has given you license to generate those inviting incentives more creatively and effectively than ever before.

At the same time, however, as a new-generation marketer, savvy in the ways of technology, can you completely walk away from what traditional marketing has taught us and accomplished? Can you dismiss the experience garnered by the wizened graybeards who have seen a zillion trends come and go and have been able to learn from their successes and failures? Can you allow online functionality to stand completely alone without any semblance of traditional support? We think not. Extreme thinking is not the answer. Smart thinking is.

New technologies have created new opportunities to reach your customers in ways you never thought possible, as well as in old-fashioned ways that now are more effective and productive.

Interactive promotional marketing has never had the possibilities it has today. And tomorrow will create even more chances for success – for those prepared to embrace the changes that have come and are coming.

Today it is no longer a matter of implementing the clichéd "outside-the-box" thinking. It's a matter of exploding the box altogether and doing away with it.

That's what we – and other venturesome companies – have been doing with interactive promotional marketing that reaches, touches, engages and motivates the consumer. We're talking about interactive games, sweepstakes, contests – relevant incentives that speak directly to the consumer and lead to a connection with the brand. These strategies and tactics have produced significant, positive results and in some cases, literally changed the way marketers are doing business. Interactive promotions have generated higher "click-throughs" to online stores, increased "tell-a-friend" referrals and buzz among colleagues and boosted opt-in rates, SMS (Short Message Service) messages and online registrations. We've gotten better direct mail response and stronger sales from our promotion entrants and improved prospect-to-customer conversion rates. It's all documented, too. We can measure these things, but we can't reveal the numbers here because they're already outdated (and they're confidential) and they show every sign of changing – for the better.

That's why you will find this book obsolete. And important. And timely. Welcome to the New World of Marketing.

CHAPTER 1:

The Digital Revolution:
Have you been paying attention?

The Digital Revolution was as life-changing as the Agricultural Revolution and the Industrial Revolution. Each of those fundamentally altered our global society.

The Digital Revolution has done nothing less. It's influence and effect has been pervasive. It has given us new ways to access information and new ways to connect with each other. Most important: it has given us ideas, stretched our imagination and taught us that what we thought was impossible is merely difficult and getting easier all the time. All because of the technology that has spawned – and been spawned by – the Revolution.

The Digital Revolution, which has changed the way we do business, shop, travel, learn, entertain, communicate, literally changing our lives, is over. It's not *happening*. It's *happened*. And it has had its shock on all of us. What we are now experiencing is the residue of its impact in almost everything we do. We haven't even felt half of what it will probably allow in the future.

What's happening now and what will be coming are the refinements, the nuances of change that will further open our eyes and minds to new ways of moving forward, *leaning forward* on all fronts in our lives. As marketers, that includes all our interactive sales and promotional efforts.

Please don't misunderstand. We are not saying there aren't more marketing (or other) revolutions waiting in the wings. No one is suggesting we close the United States Patent Office (which, as legend has it, was once proposed when it was thought that everything that could be invented had been invented). What we are saying is that until the next radical or remarkable technological, scientific breakthrough or revolution comes along, chances are the future will belong to those who recognize what the Digital Revolution has given us, follow the path it has opened and improve, enhance and capitalize on the tools and opportunities it has provided.

Future historians will look back and place the Digital Revolution and the Digital Age it sparked as starting somewhere in the late-20th Century. It probably began with the development of the first computers in the late 1930s/early 1940s and really took off in the late 1970s and '80s as computers became "PCs" and began establishing themselves as exotic, but never-the-less useful, household appliances.

From then on, it was free flight into innovation and applications unimagined outside of high-tech laboratories. Everyone knew computer technology would change things; what we perhaps didn't realize then was how dramatic and comprehensive the impact of microprocessors and the changes they allowed would be.

Suddenly computer technology wasn't limited to computers. It was everywhere. The technology and the microchips that were spewing out of Silicon Valley were invading our lives at every level. The new technology was controlling not just elite computers, it was changing audio and video, and even toasters and shavers and automobiles and air travel and home construction and manufacturing and you-name-it. Suddenly there was a software program or application for everything and anything.

It's enough to say for the moment that the invention of digital technology and the remarkable economy and efficiency of it became readily apparent through its many applications. Not only were we into the Revolution, as a result, we were also into the Information Age. Well and good. Information was suddenly more accessible than it had ever been.

What a great opportunity that presented for marketers.

But what did all this mean for interactive marketing? What was all this technology going to do for the marketer? For the brand? And for the consumer?

Good and important questions. Let's take a brief look first at the way the technology affected our evolving business capabilities and sensibilities.

CHAPTER 2:

The Digital Revolution: This is how it started

The Digital Revolution started slowly and then exploded. As the Internet and the World Wide Web were being birthed, there were hints of the upcoming blast off, again, if you were paying attention.

For example, if you walked through a large marketing research company in the mid-1980s, you would still see typewriters on people's desks and, as a recent development, dedicated CRTs with keyboards for very specific tasks (e.g., data entry, creation of documents) representing a significant initial investment and probably a huge savings efficiency in terms of hours and dollars. Of course, there were still all those stacks of files sitting around collecting dust.

In one of those offices there might have been an early personal computer. This machine would have some package of integrated software programs that allowed a user to do word processing and some useful database development. (And because this machine was so advanced and "delicate" and expensive, access to it was often limited to the more "competent" people.)

If you looked hard, you might see a curious, ambitious employee staying around after hours trying to figure out how to use those programs to create an electronic version of the card catalog that filled the walls in the same room that contained the computer. That young worker might have had the foresight to envision a future connectivity to other machines – to other sources of information – in a free-flowing network of data that could run in a number of directions. If so, that worker would have been regarded as an Early Adopter, perhaps even an Insanely Early Adopter. And if that employee was involved in direct marketing, the wheels might already be turning in that promotional direction. That employee might have been thinking: how can I use this new technology and its machines to reach, talk to and connect with my customers?

In the mid-90s, as email, centralized data storage/retrieval and commonized business software became more of the norm across businesses (enterprise-wide applications), some innovative users started to see opportunities to create efficiencies more directly linked to their daily and often narrow responsibilities. In other words, we started to see how we could leverage the technology so that available applications could positively affect our specific goals and enhance our productivity: *We could do our jobs faster and better.*

At the same time that Microsoft Windows became commonplace and Microsoft Office became ubiquitous, there arose opportunities to build very specific products (sales wizards, templates, etc.) based on tools that people in the organization already had, already knew and used and already had accepted. Although there might have been glitches here and there and competition between Macs and PCs, the handwriting was on the wall in large, clear script: "Change is coming, pal, whether you like it or not."

In those early days, these opportunities were seen in products that were Windows- based, but still pre-Internet. They included CD-ROM, CDi technology and other laser disc offerings. The first glimmerings of technologically-advanced interactive marketing were peeking through.

Many such tools supported sales and training efforts in large companies, but what they were missing was a large, reliable and fast communications infrastructure that could disseminate the data and keep the content updated, an *Intranet.*

What many of the users of the time didn't realize was that what they would eventually be using would be a pre-cursor to the systems that would determine their success or failure in interactive marketing. It was a time of great experimentation in using pre-interactive technology. Something was out there, but few knew exactly what it was or how to use it. It was almost like powerful, revolutionary cars waiting for the new expressway to open and the return of cheap gas to fuel their drives. Some would surge, some would stall. Of course, there would also be no speed limits.

Then it came, the Big Idea: the Web site.

"Everybody needs a Web site . . . Build it and your brand will be successful, and we will be able to measure your success." That was the mantra of the mid-'90s. That's what it was like as the Internet hit; the World Wide Web was the Answer and every business needed a Web site if for no other reason than the other guy had one. Best part, you were told, you'll have numbers to tell you exactly how successful you are. Well, not exactly.

Many companies fell into what we now may understand was a marketing trap or detour: a new s"sales channel" of Web sites was born and put to use without really knowing how to use it, or not being able to use it effectively because the technology wasn't quite there yet.

Early marketing on the Internet and Web sites was very similar to the advertising that took place when commercial television was introduced and spread in the late '40s/early '50s. Everyone wanted to advertise, but didn't exactly know how. In the beginning then, advertisers simply took their radio commercials and added pictures (much like what the early television shows themselves were). It took a while for them to realize television added an entirely new dimension; it wasn't just radio with pictures. Television allowed them to do things with a mass audience they could never do before, i.e., visual product displays, product demonstrations, product comparisons. You get the picture (pardon the pun). Marketers saw a mass audience waiting to be advertised to. Pretty much the way television still works today.

Looking back (don't we love hindsight?) we might ask: How many people recognized the potential of the Internet, but were relegated to only sounding smart because they knew 20 key terms no one else did? And how many were frustrated because the technology wasn't quite where they wanted – needed – it to be and didn't even realize it?

The early jargon was assigned to sales people (they were called "Internet Strategists") who could turn a Web trends report into a beautiful pie chart without making that data any more meaningful than the pretty pie chart it was.

People were looking for meaning, trying to be smart, sometimes succeeding and often failing, trying to figure out what all this budding connectivity meant. If they were marketers, they were especially asking what it would do for their brand. Some marketers were insightful enough to catch a glimpse of what the Internet and Web sites could offer: access and – if you were serious – primitive metrics.

Suddenly you would be able to – people thought – figure out which half of your advertising budget you were wasting. It was a marketer's dream: offering yourself to your target market and finding out how effective you were in doing it. Accurate measurement was born and taking shape. Eureka!

But not quite. The "connection" wasn't all there.

Keep something in mind, however: not every marketer was thrilled over the rise of the Internet. While many were perceptive enough to know something big was happening, many just wished it would go away. As one executive at an unnamed, very large automotive advertising agency said back then, "How can I care about the Internet when it generates 1% of my revenue and the other stuff kicks in 99%?" Not an uncommon view, but one that particular executive held a little too long. He's now singing a different tune, on the unemployment line.

As we got closer to Y2K and the impending worldwide blackout that never materialized, we were also seeing more and more companies rise on an Internet-only model. The spirit was intoxicating, the people were delirious and the venture capital money was being printed in basements off cheap inkjet color printers. We were all going to be billionaires and the world would change overnight. It almost did.

In that environment where high-tech companies were "dog-friendly," covered elective surgeries, offered millions in stock options and gave six weeks of vacation to new employees, one could look around and notice lots of 24-year-old software engineers who had only voted once (if they bothered), did not remember a president before Bill Clinton, believed they would retire on their stock options before age 30 and had never experienced an economic downturn. Boy, were things about to suck or what?

And they did. They really, really sucked.

When the tech bubble burst, an air of sobriety dropped Internet-related businesses out of cyberspace and back to earth. But even though some companies failed and a lot of people took severe financial gas, the technology itself was still advancing, still moving ahead and still creating opportunities for savvy marketers who had the gumption to stay with it and work to discover what the Internet could offer.

Now it was time to see what this embryonic industry really was made of. Most marketers knew the Internet was still for real. But no one was ready to throw caution to the wind. Instead, focused visionary marketers were warily preparing to take it seriously and ask that all-important question: "Okay, Internet, what can you do for me?"

The answer? Quite a bit, actually.

CHAPTER 3:

The Digital Revolution:
What happened?

Let's back up a bit before we go exploring the positive impact of the Internet on interactive marketing – or, as it may turn out, the impact of interactive marketing on the Internet.

Let's think for a minute about what the Digital Revolution ride was really all about. Yes, it was about technology. Yet, it was more than that: it was technology applied. Technology that changed the way we do things, how we communicate with each other, how we entertain ourselves, how we shop, how we work, how we bank and invest and travel, in short, literally how we conduct our lives and the business of living.

The real importance of the technology that both generated and came out of the Digital Revolution was not the technology itself. What was important was what the technology did to us culturally. It changed almost everything.

Some small examples: think about how you make phone calls now. Land lines? Ancient history. Satellite, Internet and cell phones are it. But those cell phones are not just for phone calls anymore. Those little wonders you hold in your hand keep you connected. Everything from text messages to music downloads to the latest news to email to the Internet to photos and, yes! – even advertising messages flow into that razor-thin apparatus you program and carry in your pocket or purse or briefcase. You are in touch almost everywhere you go. And just wait until you see what's around the corner!

Another example, a little more specific: the car shopping experience. Think about how you buy or lease a car these days. Once upon a time the dealer was the first stop on your shopping expedition. You'd pick up a brochure for the model that interested you, read it, look at the pretty pictures, drive the car and strike a (painful) deal with the salesperson. Today, the dealership is the last stop, maybe for a test drive or simply to pick up your vehicle. By the time you're there, you've already loaded yourself with information from perhaps a dozen Web sites. You're already familiar with your preferred model's specs. You've chosen the color and options. You know the sales price and the dealer's invoice price. You know how much you should pay. Maybe you've already even bought the car through a Web site. All because technology enables you.

Now we can buy almost anything we want online. We can study almost anything online. We can see almost anything we want. It is almost a fantasy.

Best Practice:

Online activity drives offline behavior. Recognize how the two relate to each other.

The Internet and its unlimited capacity for Web sites and communication is a marketer's dream – a canvas waiting to be painted with the messages you want your customer to receive. Even better, it's a canvas that can tell you how many people took a look at your painting. And it can paint a different picture for different types of customers.

With television, radio, print and direct marketing and all the other traditional forms of marketing and promotions, you can only guess or estimate how many consumers were exposed to your message. Yes, you can measure how much you sent out or spent, but you can never be sure of how many people actually saw, heard, read or were even interested in your message. It's all about inputs, not outcomes.

Early Web sites allowed marketers to count hits and determine the sources of those hits. But what good is a million hits a day if none of those visitors stick around for your message or dismiss it? And even if they do dive deeper into the site, do you know who they are and what they're after? It's nice to count hits, but it's not good enough. Not today. Not if you want a worthwhile ROI.

First Best Practice had:

When gathering consumer information, ask what you need and know how you will use it. If you ask questions just because you can, you make it a more cumbersome experience just to generate non-actionable data.

With interactive Internet promotional marketing done properly, precise and accurate metrics are a key part – an expected and vital part – of the marketing equation. In fact, they are a key reason for doing online interactive promotional marketing in the first place. No more shots in the dark. No more probabilities. Instead, hard numbers and lots of data that lets you refine your message and direct it more accurately and productively. More on that later.

By the way, it's important also to understand that "Online" and "Interactive" marketing are not the same things. They should not be used interchangeably. Just because it's online doesn't mean it's interactive. Online marketing can take many forms that are not interactive at all (just as interactive marketing can take many forms that are not online). Banner ads, tiles, videos, etc., do not necessarily generate the connection that defines interactive marketing. Yes, you can sometimes click through to the next level, but it isn't a two-way dialogue. It is still just plain advertising set on a Web site.

Best Practice:

Integrate interactive promotions into your advertising and direct marketing to generate stronger results. Research shows promotional banner ads generate higher click-through rates, direct mail with a promotion generates higher response rates and email with a promotional message all have higher open and response rates.

That was an early mistake a great many advertisers made: putting simple ads on a Web site. They didn't make use of what the site could do. They were using Web sites like a television set putting on commercials or ads for people to watch or read. (Many advertisers still do that.) But if consumers weren't watching them on TV or reading them in magazines, why would they do so at a Web site? Because it was a novelty? Perhaps. But that gets old fast. Granted, in some cases the technology wasn't there to allow imaginative marketers to carry out their strategies and there will always be a certain number of consumers who will look at anything (people once bought AMC Pacers and Gremlins), but this was not effective marketing.

Purposeful interactive marketing creates a one-on-one connection. Let's boldly amend that further: Nothing can generate a consumer-brand connection today the way an Internet or online promotion can. Do the right promotion the right way, attract consumers with something they want and they will gladly beat a path to your door. This is the means by which you can build that better mousetrap. You'll be able to take names and addresses *and information*. And enter the consumer's mind.

In all, the Digital Revolution precipitated and permitted a convergence of tumultuous, dissonant forces, much like worlds in collision; a dynamic gathering, if you will, of technology and marketing, branding and direct marketing, art and science, creativity and accountability. It turned the world around and gave brand advertisers an opening never before possible: a way to reach specific markets – if they knew how.

It also gave them a responsibility they never had before. Because science was now a part of the marketing effort, results could be tabulated and advertising effectiveness measured. Promotions could be evaluated with improved accuracy. The new technology was mixing oil and water and making it work, doing away with smoke and mirrors and allowing companies to demand more of their advertising agencies and marketing departments. Accountability was a pivotal factor. This was a new world of promotions and branding and if you were an ad agency or marketer that wasn't into it, you would soon be on the sidelines.

Some organizations seized on the new technology while simultaneously recognizing the forces acting on the marketplace. You'll read about the others in business-school casestudies for years to come. Adapt or die. A lesson many marketers learned – and others will learn – the hard way.

CHAPTER 4:

Interactive Marketing: a newish name for a familiar concept

So then, what is this "interactive marketing" all about? What is it really?

The concept of interactive marketing has been around for a long time under a number of aliases. It's been known as "relationship marketing," and "direct marketing" and several other pet names that brand marketers and advertising agencies created for it.

What it really is and what it boils down to is very simple: "one-on-one marketing." It's an effort by the marketer to engage the consumer by initiating a "dialogue" – creating a two-way street. While the point of such marketing is obviously to make a sale by establishing a connection between seller and buyer, the greater importance, the often-times "hidden agenda" of such an approach, is to create a relationship – a brand loyalty – that holds the two together for the long-term.

But why should such a relationship hide its intent? It can be a good thing for everyone, marketer and consumer. A successful relationship of this kind is built on mutually beneficial interests: you scratch my back, I'll scratch yours. You give me something I want at a fair price and I'll buy it. Maybe we'll even like each other along the way. Even better, maybe I'll come back to you again, and again.

Marketing relationships of this kind rely heavily on information; information that turns shoppers and prospects into consumers not just for one purchase or one shopping excursion, but for a continuing association that genuinely benefits both parties. You tell me what you're selling and why it's good. If I like it I buy it; if I don't, I tell you why and you produce a product that suits me better and I buy that instead. Engaging the consumer is what leads to this exchange and all its variables.

Best Practice:

Use an Intelligent Promotion Platform paired with dynamic content to provide consumers with the most targeted and relevant offers.

In theory, this is a great way to market and build brand loyalty. In practice, with some exceptions, it hasn't always worked that way.

Best Practice:

Use IPP to dynamically collect data from consumers and instantly give them information that interests them.

Once upon a time not so long ago, you could walk over to the corner grocery and be greeted by the store's owner, Joe, who had been there as long as you could remember. Joe knew you and your family. Usually, he'd greet you by name. "Hello, Mrs. Jones or Mr. Smith." He knew where you lived. Knew what you and your spouse and your children enjoyed eating. Sometimes he'd set aside certain items for you. "Got some nice-looking sirloin, today, Mrs. Jones. And some fresh corn, too – two for one. And I bet the kids would like the apple pie my wife baked this morning. It's on special."

You might or might not want these items. The point is, however, you had a relationship with Joe. You had a conversation. He knew what you liked and didn't like. He knew you might be in three times a week on your way home from work. He also knew the specific products and brands you wanted, and kept you informed about them. He addressed *your* needs. Because of his interest in retaining you as a customer, you went to him regularly. It worked for both of you. You could count on each other.

A lot of that went away with the advent of the supermarket. Sure, you can still get your sirloin and milk and apple pie, but does the clerk at the Wal-Mart know what you like? Do they keep you informed? Do they carry the brands you prefer? Do they pull you to the side and say "Look what just came in." Or do you have to go looking for them?

It was the same way with the salesperson, call him Bernie, who helped you shop for clothing. He knew your style, your favorite colors, that you hate – or love – plaid. Some of that goes on today (but not enough).

But how do you take that personal experience and convey it through an advertising or marketing campaign? How do you provide the personal one-on-one experience to the consumer, the kind of experience that makes them comfortable, curious, and ultimately, loyal?

Not easy. But it can be done, on a global scale like never before.

CASE STUDY

Holiday time at Dell Computers: The Dell Stocking Stuffer Promotion

Promotion overview and objectives
This was a holiday promotion directed at employees of Dell and its affiliates. Dell had three basic goals:
  _ Drive additional consideration of holiday shoppers and drive conversion to achieve ROI.
  _ Make Dell fun, cool and affordable while offering everything for a consumer's technology needs.
  _ Learn about the Employee Purchase Plan customer by asking questions at promotion registration and subsequent login questions to enable Dell to build a foundation for a future relationship with the customer.

A "stocking stuffer" game was created to stimulate participation.

How it worked

Upon registering for the promotion, site visitors were asked a number of questions regarding their interests. They were then able to select a stocking stuffed with an offer. The offers were based on questions answered during registration. If an offer was accepted, participants were emailed promotional codes and discount details. Registrants were presented with up to three discount offers per day which they could accept or reject. With each return visit, participants were asked more questions which allowed for tailoring subsequent offers to that individual's interest and thereby building the one-on-one relationship. Participants were also offered the opportunity to opt-in for additional exclusive email offers and discounts.

Key results

57% of users who viewed the pre-registration page went on to register for the promotion. This is a high conversion rate which indicates users were interested in the promotion and engaged with the Dell brand. In addition, 48% of the participants chose to opt-in for the exclusive offers – almost double the average opt-in rate for an electronics promotion. The average participant returned to the site 2.6 times. And, as Dell learned, all that computes very nicely.

For the longest time, advertisers really didn't know how to create effective personalized interactive – or for that matter, non-interactive – marketing. So they ignored it. They didn't give it the attention it deserved because, frankly, there was more money to be made in traditional advertising and it was a lot more fun what with all the trips for commercial shoots and the freebies, parties and event tickets the media sellers provided. In addition, a huge and complex infrastructure was in place to support traditional advertising. Significant investments had been made in the development of media channels. It's not easy to completely or partially walk away from "how things have always been done." This was the way things were and the way they would continue. Who wanted to waste their time on one-off marketing approaches that were questionable?

For all those reasons, traditional marketing was not going away. However, direct marketing as it was known, even though it was the bastard step-child of the industry, was lucrative and effective – to a degree – but not very glamorous. It was where the "B" team operated. After all, with the real money in broadcast and print, that's where the "A" players were placed to generate profits for the agency. The B-team could handle the direct marketing. It wasn't going to go up or down if the A-team was involved, so why bother?

However, little by little, advertisers and agencies realized relationship marketing could pay off. Direct marketing gained respect. Major ad agencies began to see some of their business – and their talent – being siphoned off by highly specialized companies that focused on direct marketing – with an A-team that made a difference – and so they created competitive, dedicated direct marketing departments. They recognized the opportunity for the one-on-ones they wanted lived in direct marketing. They just didn't know how to make it work on a broader scale.

When the Internet and Web sites kicked in, the same major agencies began to establish departments to create that form of marketing. Web marketing, too, was regarded as a step-child to the traditional. The people who worked in that department frequently were not well-versed in the ways of marketing and advertising – they were designers and programmers and tech geeks, people able to cope with the new technology and hired to do the groundwork for the coming evolution, whenever that might be – and many early Web sites were at best ineffectual and at worst counter-productive in developing consumer confidence and brand relationships. Most were filled with what became known as "brochure ware," print materials adapted to the Web. Borrring.

What wasn't well known at the time (the mid-'90s) was that the Internet and direct marketing were headed toward a friendly collision and, with some modifications, into a highly productive collaboration.

Direct marketing initially took the form of direct mail. It brought in results. But when all the costs were added up – name and address lists, postage, creative development, printing and administration – yielding a positive response of 1% (which is regarded as high), the question of "was it really worth it?" arose. In most cases, it was just enough to defend continuation of direct mail programs. Why? Because it got the brand name out there and usually contained special offers which got sufficient response from certain consumers to make the marketing effort worthwhile.

Best Practice:

Use an IPP to identify and distinguish your best prospects to provide offers that make sense for them.

But there's the rub: Which consumers? Who wanted the $1-off coupon and who would go for the $5.00 lube job and who was tempted by a three-day weekend at a Florida resort? And what did this "blinking-lights-in-your-face" approach do to the integrity of the brand?

Qualifying the target market was tricky at best. It was done by ZIP codes and area codes and a range of demographic criteria culled from public and semi-private sources. Consequently, advertisers saturated a market only to endure waste and disappointing results. Even if you knew Mr. Jones lived in a four-bedroom house in Suburbia, had a wife, three kids, two cars and a labradoodle, made $150K per year and was born in Fort Lauderdale, that didn't tell you whether he preferred Coke or Pepsi, Fords or Chevrolets, jazz or classical, Scotch or cognac. And he may have been tossing all your direct mail pieces into the trash anyway. How could you get the information needed to make direct mail more effective and Mr. Jones a customer?

Same thing when marketers discovered you could advertise on the Web. Initially, all those banner ads and tiles and search results generated hits – lots of them – but who were those people and why weren't they staying around the site? Mr. Jones wasn't giving anyone a whole lot of information about himself.

Maybe it was because every time a marketer approached Mr. Jones, it was a "push" tactic; intrusive and usually unwelcome (like TV commercials at the wrong time). And maybe, just maybe, it was because no one ever really asked properly.

Wouldn't it be nice if things were a little different? Wouldn't it be nice if you knew more substantive, specific facts about Mr. Jones? That he hates SUVs, loves the Capital Grille, rents DVDs from Netflix, shops at the Gap, drinks LaBatt's, prefers Diana Krall over Barbara Streisand, runs 15 miles a week in Reebok gear rain or shine, has accounts at Citibank, flies Northwest Airlines almost exclusively, watches ESPN, catches the news on his Palm PDA and does all his banking, travel planning, book and music shopping online.

Best of all, wouldn't it be even nicer if Mr. Jones said, "Sure, I'd love to hear about your products. Here's what I'm interested in."

A marketer's dream or what? Exactly what ePrize has been doing for clients for years.

CHAPTER 5:

"Push" advertising is being pushed away

Frankly, most people today do not want to be bothered with intrusive advertising. In their hearts, marketers have always known that. It's just been difficult to admit or accept. The thinking has been: beat the consumer over the head often enough and eventually he just might relent and buy your product. But is that the way a quality brand wants to go? Does that really build loyalty or goodwill? And what does that say about your brand's strength? (Or weakness?) About brand equity and integrity? In the end is the purchase just a purchase or the start of a relationship?

Consumer backlash is having its impact.

For the longest time, interactive marketing was not the most important advertising channel. Advertisers preferred – and most still do – to thrust their commercials and ads at consumers through conventional means. Traditional marketing, including direct advertising, has always been about "push" – pushing the message at the consumer. Commercials would come *at* consumers. And consumers fought back.

Any number of sources will show you traditional advertising channels no longer work the way they once did. People just don't trust advertising the way they once – if ever – did. With VCRs, people realized they could video-tape their entertainment to watch it when they wanted to, not when the programmers told them to.

When DVRs and TIVO were developed, the process became smoother and more sophisticated. "Okay, Mr. TV Executive, I'll watch your show because I do enjoy it, but I'll watch it on a Sunday afternoon when I have 48 minutes free and not on Thursday nights when I bowl or I'm busy or simply too zonked to bother. Oh, and by the way, when I do watch it, I'll be skipping the commercials."

Not exactly a marketer's dream results.

Yet, that's just part of it. Drivers now tune out AM and FM radio stations in favor of CD players and satellite programming. Newspaper readers get their information off the Internet. Magazines emphasize their Web sites more than newsstand sales. Even Internet and email ads are tuned out through pop-up blockers and spam filters. Consumers are turning away from the advertising they don't want because they don't have to accept it anymore. Research shows fully 75% of them are interested in how they can block television, radio and Internet advertising.

And don't forget that little thing known as "The Do-not-call" list. Most of us aren't hounded by telemarketers these days – an 80% sign-up rate has been reported. Another channel shut down, much to the chagrin of many credit card companies and local construction firms. "Don't bother me!" is the consumer declaration.

Could the message be any clearer? Consumers are turning away from intrusive, irrelevant marketing *because they can.*

Reality also says consumers don't have enough time these days to see or read everything marketers want them to. You can't watch "Lost" and "Desperate Housewives" and "CSI: Whatever" as well as read the local newspaper, *The New York Times, Sports Illustrated, Maxim, The New Yorker, Wired, Vogue* and *Runner's World* and go to work and spend time with your friends and family. It's all too much.

Consumers have a lot of choices and they're showing a distinct preference for making them on their terms – not yours. They make those choices through the inventions that came from the Digital Revolution, through computers and Web sites and through those little, hand-held cell phones and PDAs. Consumers are enthusiastically exercising their right to say "No, thank you." And there's only so much you can do about it.

Marketers, however, still need to contact consumers. As a result, advertisers are almost desperate in their attempts to reach the public. And it shows. Almost anywhere you look, you'll see advertising. The branding phenomena has permeated our lives. Desperate to scream louder and stand taller, big brands are buying naming rights to sports stadiums and events, concert halls, theatres, even urinals; placing their products in movies and theatrical productions, anything for brand recognition. Often this strengthens brand awareness, but then, again, how do you know? And what does this do beyond basic brand recognition? Does it build resentment ("Why are you everywhere I go? Hustling me when I'm at the movies? I'm paying ten bucks to see a movie, NOT your ads.") or loyalty? Does it translate into sales of more soap or cars or beer or music or clothing? "Maybe" to all of these questions. But wouldn't you want to be certain?

Most of these mass marketing and advertising efforts are targeted at people who remain anonymous. Sure, marketers would like to go one-on-one with consumers, but these methods don't allow it. These are what we call "broadcast thinking" which means literally talking to the lowest common denominator. The efforts are intended to reach the broadest audience possible. It's a saturation/shotgun approach that includes an enormous amount of waste. The results are generally disappointing because you're talking mostly to people who aren't listening in the first place or tuning out your message as soon as they realize it isn't addressed to them. The process is inefficient, the return, though sometimes acceptable, could be much better with other techniques.

So doesn't it make sense to get on the good side of consumers?

Best Practice:

Think about the consumer. Give them a reason to interact with your brand.

We've found the opposite approach works far better: know your target market and provide them with marketing tactics they are ready to accept based on the information they have already provided to you. It's called "permission marketing," and it works.

Permission marketing is commonly used in current marketing strategies by Internet, email and telephone marketers. The idea is to ask permission before you send advertising to a prospective customer. It works on the basis of people "opting in" to receive advertising rather than "opting out" after the advertising has been sent. The rationale is that this is a better use of marketing dollars because the people opting in are more receptive to the message and resources aren't wasted on people who have no interest in what you're selling.

Traditional advertising works on the hope of stealing your attention away from whatever you're doing to get you to listen to a sales message. It's interruptive and, as many companies have realized, usually not productive and often counter-productive, turning people off to your brand. As Seth Godin, author of *Permission Marketing: Turning Strangers Into Friends and Friends into Customers*, puts forth, instead of annoying potential customers by interrupting them and taking up their time with something they don't want to see or hear, permission marketing offers consumers incentives – reasons – to accept advertising voluntarily. Connecting only with people interested in your message enables marketers to build relationships and brand awareness – and spend dollars that have the possibility of giving you a better ROI.

Beyond that, Godin lists the four tests of effective permission marketing:

1. Does your marketing effort encourage a learning relationship with your customers and invite them to "raise their hands" and participate?
2. Have you created a permission database and tracked the numbers of people who have accepted your invitation to communicate with them?

3. Do you have anything to say to the people who have given you permission to contact them? What are you teaching them about your product?
4. Do you work to extend the relationship you have been given permission to establish?

To put it in clear and simple terms, think of permission marketing as inviting a friend over to your house for dinner versus having someone randomly knock at your door and try to get a seat at your table. Which person would you be more receptive to? Which person would you be more excited to see?

CASE STUDY

The Smith & Hawken $5,000 Gift Card Giveaway

Promotion overview and objectives
Smith & Hawken, outdoor furniture and gardening equipment retailer, wanted to increase its prospective customer base. They elected to conduct a promotion in which they gave away a $5,000 gift card. With this interactive promotion and attractive prize, they hoped to increase:
  _ Acquisitions of new customers and their address data
  _ Email sign-ups with address information
  _ Site traffic, referrals and overall brand awareness

How it worked
Visitors to the promotion splash page were given the chance to win the $5,000 Gift Card Giveaway. All they had to do was register to win. They could return once a day to see if they were a winner. They were also given the choice of opt-in to receive more information about Smith & Hawken products via email. Essentially they were giving Smith & Hawken permission to contact them in the future. Further, participants were given the option to tell-a-friend about the promotion – and they did.

Key results

The promotion was effective: registrations were high with participants returning to the Web site an average of 6.38 times. Return on investment was significant with marketing dollars spent on a highly-targeted and responsive audience rather than the broad target – most of which may well be uninterested in this particular brand's offering – a mass media campaign would be directed to. Every one of those visits presented a selling opportunity for Smith & Hawken. In addition, 62% of the registrants gave their permission to receive more information. And, of those who registered, 44% provided tell-a-friend referrals and, in turn, 14% of those entered the promotion. Great numbers for the great outdoors.

People respond to interactive marketing that offers them reasons – incentives – to act or react. They are given something of value they want to check out.

Through effective use of incentivized promotional marketing, games and sweepstakes, we gain the consumer's permission to advertise to them. We give them a good enough reason to allow us in the door and in return they willingly give us the information needed for productive future contact. In fact, 82% of consumers* are willing to provide personal information in exchange for the chance to win.

This is what our clients have found succeeds for them. And our clients are some of the most successful brands in the business.

This is not the same as pure "brand advertising." Brand advertising is an effort to strengthen awareness and is intended to create favorable images of the brand. The hoped-for resulting recognition and good feeling about the brand is intended to nurture loyalty and drive the consumer to

---

* Jupiter Research, 2003

continually choose that brand over another one. Sometimes it works, sometimes it doesn't.

Promotional/direct marketing can build brand awareness and image, too, but it tries to do even more: it works to produce a specific response, a specific behavior; that could be a sale of a certain item or service, a visit to a dealership or store or some other desired act. In effect, it's a trade of sorts: we'll do this if you do that. Traditional marketing does this, too, but interactive promotions go one better: they work through one-to-one marketing to offer incentives for the consumer to identify with – and even *involve* himself – with the brand.

That in a nutshell is what interactive promotional marketing is and does. ePrize has refined this approach to a sophisticated and highly effective level that accomplishes the short-term goal of brand awareness and supports it with genuine respect for the consumer to subsequently establish long-term loyalty. Two for the price of one. And it works.

For obvious reasons, long-term consumer relationships are important. When a car dealer sells an SUV to a customer, ideally, it would be good for the dealer if the consumer kept coming back for all future vehicle and service needs. Toward that end, the dealer might try to stay in touch with the customer and provide exceptional service whenever the customer comes back for vehicle maintenance or repair. Maybe the dealer would distribute discount coupons to the customer to lure them back for oil changes or tune-ups or brake jobs or even a deal on the next car. The whole point would be to continue the relationship.

Best Practice:

Any time you want to motivate specific behavior or solicit information, provide the consumer with an incentive to achieve the desired objective.

The same principle applies to supermarkets, hotels, department stores, airlines and even Web sites. But in the example above, where is the two-way dialogue needed to elicit information that allows the dealer to gather the knowledge that makes the relationship grow?

True, the dealer is giving the customer some value, but what is the dealer learning about the customer that could be even more valuable? There may be some sort of customer survey, but those are generally questions about the dealership or the product or the service. The customer's opinion is valued. But where are the questions from the dealer *about the customer and what the customer wants?* The dealer is only learning about his own operation. What is the dealer learning about the customer? What is the dealer learning that will give him the information he needs to ensure future customer visits by offering the customer compelling reasons to return?

There is a way. This is where interactive marketing takes a promotional direction and yields the results the marketer wants and the consumer is ready to provide.

CHAPTER 6:

What can be done . . . and what we've learned

If there is such a thing as the perfect or near-perfect promotional medium, online interactive is it. Time and again, we have seen how versatile it can be. It's multitude of capabilities applied imaginatively has driven positive measurable results repeatedly for ePrize clients.

That success is understandable and almost inevitable.

Think about this: according to *CBS Sunday Morning*, consumers today are exposed to a daily dose of approximately 5,000 ads. In the '70s, it was about 500 per day. It's more media than ever before and it's everywhere you turn. Consumers can't process all the data thrown at them. They have relationships with about 20 different brands – brands they prefer and buy regularly. Everything else is peripheral, occasional and devoid of loyalty. Advertisers are scrambling to find a captive audience. So the question is, how do you cut across all that clutter and noise without alienating the consumer? How does a struggling marketer working to gain entry to the consideration area of the consumer's mind get on the radar screen? To put it in blunt, capitalistic terms, how in the world do you get the consumer to notice you, become engaged, pull out his wallet and go from prospect to customer?

Best Practice:

Put the consumer first. What do they get for talking to you? Don't fool yourself into thinking they want to spend time with your brand just because you're a big name company. There are lots of big name companies out there.

Even better, given all the competition today for the consumer's dollar (and attention), how do you get the consumer to choose your computer not just over another company's computer, but also over something completely different? Like a weekend in the Bahamas? The competition is no longer just another brand, it could be a whole other product or service *outside your category.* If we're talking about disposable income and discretionary spending, will the consumer choose a new plasma TV or a trip to Europe? A new car or a new fancy backyard deck? It isn't just apples to apples anymore. There are lots of things to buy. How do you get your voice heard? Your product considered? How do you differentiate within your own category *and* succeed against other categories?

Yes, it's tricky, but it's not all that difficult.

Remember the movie "The Graduate?" (You might be too young, go get the DVD. It was good.) The word to success then was "plastics." I suggest an updated two-word version: "interactive promotions."

Web-based interactive promotions consist of everything from sweepstakes, games, incentives, loyalty programs, coupons and – as advertisers love to say – "much, much more," with each being a branding opportunity. The way interactive promotions work is by attracting the attention of the consumer and then retaining it through a value exchange – giving something to get something (more on that in a few pages). By engaging the consumer in a voluntary (emphasis on "voluntary") marketing tactic, you have a much better chance of the consumer listening/seeing/getting your message. The consumer becomes an active and willing participant rather than a passive observer. In effect, the consumer is *leaning forward,* voluntarily receptive to your message.

Now step back for a second and think about this fundamental precept: The only thing advertising or marketing can really do is persuade you to consider a certain product or service. It generally can't sell you something you don't want. But the more persuasive the message, the better the chance for consideration, request for more information and the ultimate sale.

So how do you persuade the consumer to choose your product?

First, you've got to get his attention. If you can't do that, you certainly can't get him to listen to your message. But even if you get his attention, will he listen to your message, and if he does will he remember it and will he act on it?

Go back to Joe the grocery store shopkeeper or Bernie, the salesman where you buy your suits. When Joe made a suggestion, you thought about it. You didn't always buy, but you listened to what he said. Same thing when Bernie called you to tell you about the new fall sweaters. They *knew* you. You had an ongoing *relationship* with them. You trusted them because what they spoke to you about was generally relevant to your needs and interests. If not, you simply wouldn't shop there anymore. Interactive promotions have that potential. They allow marketers to develop those kinds of relationships.

Would I tell you that going to a Web site will create the same intimate relationship a consumer has with a Joe or Bernie? No, I won't insult your intelligence, but I will tell you that technology allows a consumer and marketer to build a relationship based on designated preferences and a knowledge of what the consumer is not only willing to accept, but eager to find. The real gem is the ability now to do it to an audience of millions.

That bond isn't built overnight, however. Like any relationship it takes time and trust to develop and define itself. And it must advance, moving ahead with every contact. It's like dating. Yes, it really is.

Think about the usual first date. More than likely, you're not going to ask your date to marry you. That's rushing things just a bit. If you're like most people, the date consists of light conversation, a search for compatibility and common ground. What you learn determines whether or not you'll get together again and, if so, builds a basis for the next meeting. You might ask your date where he or she works, for example. What her interests are. You're collecting bits of data at a time

as you build a relationship. That's exactly what interactive promotions does – on a global scale.

Continuing with the dating analogy, a consumer's relationship with a brand has a better chance of growing as the
two get to know each other. That happens as time and trouble
is taken to learn about each other. That's the beauty of interactive promotions, it allows that opportunity. (Of course,
every time there's a "date," you better not be asking the very
same questions or you won't be learning anything new and
your date won't hang around very long.) Consumers are
offered the games and contests they enjoy playing. Marketers
make it worth their while to enter into a relationship with a
brand and once a connection is made, the relationship is
dynamically advanced so that as the consumer gains brand
information and gives personal data, the dialogue becomes
more tailored.

Using what's known as an Intelligent Platform Promotion
(IPP™), a marketer can learn more about the consumer and
instantly act on it. As the consumer responds to questions,
IPP dynamically uses that information to take the consumer
down an appropriate, ever refined path. IPP has the ability to
dynamically present screens based on the consumer's
responses. IPP also remembers the information it accumu-
lates and aggregates it over time to build a relationship for the
marketer. IPP deepens that relationship – both long-term and
short-term. If we think of it in dating terms, not having IPP in
dating would be like not listening to or remembering anything
your date says and always starting out as if you were on a first
date with the same person. That's no way to build a long-term
relationship.

Best Practice:

*Use IPP and you won't need to ask the same question twice – and
you'll be able to use the answer immediately.*

CASE STUDY

Quicken Loans $10,000 Cash Giveaway

Promotion overview and objectives

Quicken Loans, a leading national mortgage company, was eager to develop a promotion that would achieve several objectives:

- *Grow online marketing channels*
- *Create a hand-raisers databank for future marketing*
- *Drive traffic to www.quickenloans.com*

They elected to create a giveaway, or "sweepstakes," promotion with a grand prize of $10,000, as well as a generous number of "instant win" prizes that included gift cards and movie tickets.

How it worked

The sweepstakes and instant win promotion ran for four weeks. Site visitors were invited to register for the promotion and then fill out a consumer survey of questions (an option). Participants were asked to opt-in and were given several choices regarding their interest in the type of information they wanted from Quicken Loans.

The response to the questions, an Intelligent Platform Promotion Survey functionality, determined which screen the participant would see next. This also allowed Quicken to learn, over time, more about the consumer. After registering and completing the survey, the participant had a chance to win an instant prize. In addition, the consumer could also tell-a-friend about the promotion and, if desired, even arrange for a mortgage expert contact.

Key results

The most notable result was that on average, registrants entered the promotion site 10.5 times, greatly exceeding the industry average of 2 – 4 times. In addition, the average tell-a-friend referrals per participant were 2.66, almost double the financial industry range. An intelligent promotion, indeed.

On behalf of our clients, we at ePrize give consumers a chance for a trip, a car, music, clothing. In exchange, we ask them to answer questions about themselves or to refer us to a friend ("viral" marketing) or give us an opinion. Along the way, we learn more about them, about what they like, why they came to the Web site. We respond to that – and expand the audience and the marketing opportunities that opening allows. The technology today can tailor Web sites and incentives to the individual based on the information they have willingly, even enthusiastically provided. Each time they return to the site, they are greeted by a page that's more focused at them than on the previous visit because all the data they've provided has been incorporated to create an experience that will appeal to them. Two people playing a Coca-Cola or Adidas game will start off on the same Web page, but as they play, the second page they see will be altered to reflect their initial responses and individual interests, tastes and preferences. That customization continues and is refined with every subsequent page and visit, producing an ongoing, customized, individual experience.

That is a critical and essential difference between interactive promotions and mass marketing. When was the last time you saw a TV commercial produced expressly for you? But, in effect, that can be done through online promotions.

I'm going to give you some more examples of what can be created, executed and achieved with interactive promotions, but first let me provide you with the objectives these promotions allow. Here's a comprehensive list of what our experience (and metrics) can accomplish and deliver (categorized in buckets):

Create New Brand Touch Points
- Create multiple touch points
  - A touch point is every way a consumer interacts with a brand. Interactive promotions represent a new touch point for brands to connect with consumers.

- Extend brand reach (internationally and domestically)
  - Reach more people (the right targeted people). Different communication vehicles reach different groups of consumers and interactive promotions provide a new communication platform to extend a brand's reach.
- Extend online reach
  - Reach more people (the right targeted people). Interactive promotions cut through the online clutter and engage consumers with your brand.
- Produce partner introductions
  - Many companies have similar targets, marketing objectives and key selling seasons. Interactive promotions allow synergy to be generated and relationships to be built around them resulting in increased effectiveness, efficiency and reach.

Brand Engagement
- Develop on-going one-on-one relationships
  - Not just one-time promotional activities that build, customize and strengthen relationships over time.
- Create brand immersion experiences
  - A deeper "active" marketing experience vs. traditional "passive" marketing interactions (television, print, radio, etc).
- Develop innovative strategies
  - Helps you stand out and get noticed versus "me too" marketing. Also, brands with innovative marketing are seen as innovative brands – keep in mind, every brand touch point reinforces the brand equity.
- Drive Web visit frequency
  - Interactive promotions can be used to increase the number of occasions a consumer visits your Web site within a given period of time. The value is an increased relationship which leads to increased branding and purchases.

- Increase Web site efficacy
  - The more you know about a consumer the better you are able to connect them to relevant parts of your Web site.

Personalized Marketing
- Pinpoint marketing efforts
  - Focus the right message on the right person at the right time rather than a "one size fits all" message.
- Market to those who are already listening
  - As opposed to pushing messages out to millions of consumers, some of whom will find it valuable and others who will be disinterested or turned off. This allows you to connect with the hand-raisers for their brand.
- Clarify differentiation at Point of Sale (POS)
  - POS (display at grocery store, retail) is a one-size-fits-all marketing approach versus the customized one-to-one online promotion. A POS can use a general message to drive consumers to an online promotion to engage in a one-to-one marketing activity.

Collect Information
- Provide clean actionable data
  - A data dump is not actionable. Collect the right data in a consistent format which can be leveraged for future marketing efforts.
- Accelerate lead generation
  - By asking the right questions in registration, capturing information and generating opt-ins, you can spawn proven leads of consumer re-marketing targets.

Education

- Stimulate product launches
  - For a product launch, use to generate deeper product awareness and understanding. If something is new, you need to educate consumers about it.
- Train, educate and reward employees
  - Interactive promotions are not just a business-to-consumer marketing strategy. The concept of providing an incentive to get someone's time, attention and, ultimately, drive a specific behavior works in the internal, company world as well.

Drive Behavior

- Build consumer retention and loyalty
  - Keep more one-time purchasers or occasional purchasers who buy on price rather than on their relationship with a particular brand.
- Drive Web site visit frequency
  - Increase the number of occasions a consumer visits your Web site within a given period of time.
- Draw immediate responses
  - Interact immediately and dynamically with users on the Web, capturing data immediately. Traditional forms of marketing don't allow this to such extent.
- Drive sales
  - Convert consumer experiences into sales through increasing brand awareness, providing a printable coupon, digital coupon, highlighting the most relevant product information, creating an ongoing relationship with the consumer, etc.
- Increase near-term purchase rates and engagement
  - Provide incentive to listen and act now.

- Increase purchase rates over long-term
  - A deeper relationship is not only about triggering a purchase at that moment. It's about that moment and on-going opportunities.
- Channel compliance
  - Ensuring that a channel executes a program correctly. Same idea as stated earlier in the "Train, educate and reward employees" section. A channel is anyplace that sells your product (i.e., a grocery store for consumer packaged goods, a big box store for an appliance or electronics manufacturer).
- Set up retail tie-in/sell-through
  - Retail customers have grown significantly in power, influence and sophistication. A strong promotion helps convince a customer that a brand is committed to investing in their product and that consumers will respond by purchasing (which, of course, benefits the retail customer). This helps sell in additional shelf space, display space, in-store and circular communication, etc. Additionally, interactive promotions provide a flexible cost-effective solution where major companies can provide individual stores with their own customer overlay promotion rather than everyone sharing the same national promotion. Big, powerful customers want that special treatment.

Consumer Generated Content
- Generate community experience
  - Create content that isn't pushed out by your brand. Let your consumers contribute to your identity and experience as well. Creates a two-way dialogue and also provides the value of having consumer testimonials as part of your marketing message.

- Spur viral marketing
  - Get users to tell their friends about your product and promotion.

Accountability
- Produce consistent results
  - The better your data, the better you can predict future activity and results.
- Establish a single point of accountability
  - Use your promotion as a "hub" for your marketing efforts. Track and measure the performance of not only your promotion, but also the other elements of the marketing mix that are driving users to the promotion.
- Maximize promotion ROI
  - By being able to provide measurement, dynamic content, drive sales, motivate behavior, etc., you can deliver the highest return on your promotional investment.
- Allow big ideas on a small budget
  - Interactive promotions offer a far more flexible and cost-efficient platform than other traditional forms of media.

The Reader's Digest version of all that would go something like this.

Interactive promotions:

- Drive immediate and measurable results to a wide range of marketing objectives
- Motivate specific behavior such as purchases, Web site visits, registrations, referrals, retail visits, coupon redemption and survey completion
- Create hand-raisers, push fence-sitters into action, establish one-on-one relationship, capture information and increase value of existing ad budgets

- Require a mix of services including strategy, creative design, cutting-edge technology for maximum effect
- Are more efficient and deliver stronger results than mass marketing approaches

Can you do all that with traditional advertising? Can you create a TV, radio or print campaign to accomplish all that? How about a traditional direct marketing campaign? With a combination of traditional media forms? We don't think so. In fact, forgive our smugness, but we know so.

It's a heckuva list. It's real and it's not just us. Those who do it right can enjoy all these things. You just have to know how. The smart marketers are either already there or learning. They understand people want a reason to pay attention. Give them that reason with incentives. They'll take you up on them. We live in a "what's-in-it-for-me" society. It's time to accept that fact and take advantage of it.

CASE STUDY

DisneyShopping.com
Pirates of the Caribbean Instant Win Game and Sweepstake

Promotion overview and objectives
DisneyShopping.com wanted to leverage the imminent release of the movie "Pirates of the Caribbean 2: Dead Man's Chest" to create a brand immersive experience that would:
 _ *Increase visits and online sales at DisneyShopping.com*
 _ *Identify and acquire new guests with a high Disney affinity*
 _ *Drive awareness of the movie launch and Pirates of the Caribbean brand*

DisneyShopping.com selected an instant win game with a sweepstakes element and an incentivized tell-a-friend section. The primary target audience was moms and Disney enthusiasts.

The secondary target was kids and "Pirates" fans. The grand prize was a trip to the Walt Disney World Resort in Florida. Instant prizes included 1,200 online DisneyShopping.com gift cards.

How it worked

Participants learned about the promotion through DisneyShopping.com and emails. Once at the promotion site and registered (and automatically entered for the grand prize), participants were taken to a Pirates of the Caribbean game page where instructions were displayed. They were then turned loose to play the :30 game. At the end of the game, they were told whether they won or lost and the number of points they accumulated. They could reach five pirate levels depending on the number of points scored. Each level also offered a printable badge. Winners were given their instant win prize. Participants could return to play again. They were also given a 10% DisneyShopping.com discount incentive for referring friends to the promotion.

Key results

Talk about pirate treasure! Participants returned to the site an average of 3.59 times – one of the highest rates for a DisneyShopping.com promotion. Also, of those who referred friends, the average person referred 2.44 people to the promotion.

Best Practice:

Do not view Interactive Promotions as a stand-alone part of a marketing plan. Different marketing vehicles can function together to drive maximum synergy, efficiency and success. An interactive promotion is a destination that requires other marketing and communication methods to drive consumers to the promotion. "If you build it, they will come" does not apply here.

Best Practice:

Any time you're competing for someone's attention or time, you need to provide an incentive. Don't kid yourself into believing they'll listen just because you have a message for them. There are many brands out there screaming for attention.

The concept doesn't apply only to individual, private consumers. Business-to-business marketers are discovering the value of interactive promotions, linking trade show exhibits with online gaming. Even employee recruiting can be positively affected by interactive promotions. We recently created a trivia game to attract CPAs to a major firm. We thought trivia and CPAs would go together. They did.

CASE STUDY

AICPA Trivia Contest Promotion

Promotion overview and objectives

The American Institute of Certified Public Accountants (AICPA) wanted to raise awareness of their profession and generate recruiting leads from business-focused college students. A game promotion was devised that included a sweepstakes win opportunity, trivia questions about the profession, instant wins and a tell-a-friend referral engine – an especially important part of the program. Three sweepstakes prizes of $1,000 each as well as instant prizes of portable DVD players and gift cards were to be awarded.

How it worked

Participants registered to play and were entered in the sweepstakes. Answering trivia questions correctly opened the door to instant prizes. Registrants could also refer up to five friends to the promotion and for each valid referral, they earned an additional entry into the sweepstakes.

Key results

This promotion was intended to reach a highly specialized niche market. Because the trivia game was accounting-based, only those friends who were genuinely qualified would have a chance to answer trivia questions correctly for a chance to win. However, the cash sweepstakes and instant win prizes were attractive enough to create a substantial referral engine data base. In fact, 3.3% of the registrants referred friends and while that may not sound like a huge percentage, it is a significant number when it applies to a specific "narrow" profession such as accounting. In fact, the AIPAC found they could count on this promotion to deliver what they wanted.

Before we get into other examples of interactive promotional success, here's another point to consider: Knowledgeable internet marketers do not live in a vacuum. Smart marketers know that as productive and efficient and effective as online promotions can be, there are situations which call for offline support and vice versa. That's why in some cases you'll see promotions that link different media forms in pursuit of an overall goal, such as Web site-generated coupons for in-store purchases or in-store promotions that drive consumers online. The critical point here is that the Internet and Web sites are finally being seen as a key element in any marketing mix, and on a more frequent basis, *the* key element.

The bottom line is about your bottom line and how to improve it. Web-based promotions are the appropriate tools for reaching today's discerning bumper crop of independent-minded consumers.

CHAPTER 7:

Playing the game

Today's technology allows us to key in more effectively than ever to human nature. Consider the average consumer. When mulling over a potential purchase, in one form or another, the consumer is always asking "What's in it for me? Is the price right? Is the product right? *What am I getting* out of this purchase, this response, this act?"

The consumer requires motivation to take action. That motivation may come from need ("I need a new dress") or desire ("I want a new iPod") or even simple curiosity ("I wonder what the new Corvette is like") or impulse ("I want a latte").

Yet, regardless of the underlying motivation, if you want the consumer to come to you for your product or service, you must somehow motivate him to choose you. You have to give him or her a reason to do that. After all, with a multitude of competing products on the market in every category, why should the consumer pick X over Y? There may be nuances of difference between two products, but there is also a lot of parity. Why select Tropicana over Minute Maid? Coke over Pepsi? Chevy over Ford? Could it be a matter of brand awareness? Brand loyalty? Experience with the product? The influence of friends and family? Perceived product superiority? All of the above? Probably the latter.

Remember Cracker Jacks? They're still around. Maybe you remember them from your kid days. Why did people like Cracker Jacks? Why were they so popular? They didn't really taste any better than other snack foods, but everyone (at least in my crowd) preferred Cracker Jacks. Why? You know why. They had a prize inside the package. A plastic car. A top. A fake tattoo. Something. A little bonus that made you reach for the Cracker Jacks instead of the Goobers or Junior Mints (although those were pretty good, too). That prize predisposed millions of people to select Cracker Jacks over the competition. As a result, Cracker Jacks stood out on the grocery shelf and distinguished themselves from the rest of the category. That little trinket inside the box was the tie-breaker that put Cracker Jacks in your shopping cart.

Cracker Jacks are a simple analogy of what promotions are all about. The promotions give knowledgeable marketers an opportunity to make contact with consumers and turn them into customers. They are a tool that allows a brand – your brand – to stand out above the noise and get your message heard. They help *differentiate* you. That differentiation can be a specific physical advantage (your paint lasts longer, your watch is more accurate) or it can be a perceived distinction (the cache of fashion, the "hot" new latte chain). The distinction makes the difference.

But what gets someone to pay attention to you, to want to know what your brand is all about? This can be done in what we call a "value exchange." It means giving the consumer a good enough reason to take their time to pay attention to you.

The value exchange is the basis for the interactive consumer/marketer relationship. The marketer wants a contact, a start to a one-on-one rapport, which is followed by consideration, a purchase, more purchases and long-term loyalty. The consumer, in turn, wants a good enough reason to stop what she's doing to even think about your product.

These days, a good product alone is not enough for the consumer in this type of exchange. That doesn't mean a consumer won't listen or be curious or interested, it just means more and more consumers are saying to marketers, "What's in it for me?" The marketer has to give them a reason. Consequently, a marketer exchanges value for the consumer's time and ultimate attention.

The value can take many forms, both tangible and intangible. The prizes offered through interactive promotions are, obviously, part of that value, as are the benefits a consumer receives from a product he likes.

And what does the marketer receive in the exchange? That's the beauty of interactive promotions and how they differentiate themselves from non-interactive programs. A properly structured interactive promotion can yield a bounty of data that sets up future interactions. In exchange for participating in your interactive promotion and receiving something of value, the consumer is giving you something of value: Information – fields and fields of information. As the relationship progresses, the consumer, in response to your questions, provides more and more data about her preferences, likes and dislikes. This data can then be used to further the relationship and generate loyalty to the brand.

It is what drives a consumer to buy a $6 cup of coffee at Starbucks over a $1.50 cup at the diner down the street. We suspect the coffee itself is only a small part of the reason for that purchase. It has a lot more to do with what the consumer perceives he receives for that $6: cache, the store's ambiance, the scene, a place to congregate, etc.

The question then is what can you, as a marketer, do to attract the consumer? How do you set yourself apart and what do you offer?

Sometimes it just takes an incredible prize, because people simply want a chance to win.

CASE STUDY

The Target Red-Hot Summer Promotion

Promotion overview and objectives

Target wanted to build brand equity and awareness through clear, creative differentiation. They were looking for a promotion that would immerse participants in the Target brand experience for a significant period of time. A sweepstakes promotion was developed that called for entrants taking part in an interactive journal with weekly challenges and a weekly sweepstakes *drawing for a new Saturn Sky sports car as well as two grand prizes consisting of the car along with $1,000 and a $500 Target gift card.*

How it worked

Participants learned about the promotion through a multimedia approach consisting of in-store and online advertising. Participants registered for the sweepstakes and were given the choice to opt-in for weekly email or mobile reminders of the promotion. They could enter once a week – without re-registering – for eight weeks. They were engaged through an interactive journal and fun challenges. They were also asked to tell-a-friend about the promotion.

Key results

When your brand gives away 10 red-hot sports cars over an eight-week period, people tend to be interested. That was the case here as Target saw great numbers of individuals registering with more than 70% of them opting in for the weekly email and mobile reminders. The tell-a-friend component was also very successful with 26.9% of the registrants referring friends. That was above the high end of the average referral rate for a promotion like this. All of which tends to demonstrate that when there's a chance to win a prize as compelling as this one, perhaps the sky is not the limit.

Research has found that 82% of consumers are willing to trade personal information for a chance to win a prize in a sweepstakes or game. It's the price they're willing to pay-to-win something of significance. Does it pay off? Absolutely – for both consumers and advertisers.

Think about Las Vegas, for example, a city built and driven by the simple concept of a "chance-to-win," and a perfect analogy of a value exchange.

When Las Vegas was first established in the desert in the middle of nowhere as the gambling capitol of the United States, crowds weren't flocking there to go hiking or take in the desolate scenery. They went there to gamble and win and have a good time doing it.

Tourists arrived hoping to come away with a pocketful of gold. Most didn't, but there were just enough winners to keep the "big jackpot" dream alive.

Along the way, related services developed. Visitors had to have lodging, food, transportation, entertainment. The hospitality industry flourished. Soon enough other peripheral services were added – all the things any growing city needs.

Loyalties also developed. Tourists had preferences as to which hotels they would stay at, which shows they wanted to see, where they wanted to eat. Whichever hotel gave the most "comped" the guests got the most. "Free" drinks, meals, rooms and more were given to preferred visitors who then gambled at that hotel's casinos. Most important, the gamblers were willing to risk money to win more money. Just as in an interactive promotion where the currency is information: I'll risk personal information, to a degree, to win the prize you're offering.

Today, Las Vegas is a metropolis with school systems, convention and recreational facilities, public services and yes, a booming tourism industry. It isn't 100% gambling anymore, but make no mistake about it. Las Vegas was born and is there – booming – because of the human desire for the chance-to-win. That's the essence of an interactive promotion.

If you have to ask do interactive promotions work, I would suggest you check the statistics from just a few of the promotions we've conducted:

- A 100-times increase in direct-mail response rates for a national retailer
- Over one million registered users in six weeks for a major airline
- Triple the qualified leads for a U.S. automotive manufacturer
- An average frequency of 20 repeat visits for a large hotel brand
- Over $1.4 million in net profit for a global electronics brand

These are real numbers. The results of giving consumers a chance to win everything from cash to trips to clothing wardrobes and more. Not only are the statistics impressive, the mere fact that they're available is impressive. You can't obtain accuracy like this through any other media form.

Internet technology allows you to track and compile all the statistical data needed to determine whether your promotion is doing what it should. Needless to say, with an interactive promotion, the cost per customer exposure is very attractive because of the potentially high ROI. The Smith & Hawken case study on page 30 is an example of ROI rewards. Instead of going for an expensive mass market broadside or scatter-gun approach that would probably reach some of their target, they would also reach a great many uninterested people (people who would find the offering irrelevant), Smith & Hawken created an interactive promotion that would target their market niche. The promotion was not as broad as mass media, but it hit the people who had a real interest in what Smith & Hawken had to say. It was fewer dollars better spent to produce a much more satisfying return.

Best Practice:

Clearly define your promotional objective and associate a defined success metric with it.

Even more attractive than pure numbers and dollars is the experience the customer has. She is engaged in your promotion! This is brand immersion at it's finest. By choosing to participate in an online promotion, the consumer is choosing to accept your messages in *your* brand environment. Granted, there is no guarantee of true loyalty, but let's be blunt: your chance for success is a whole lot better than through a TV commercial. The customer is on your Web site, focused on your brand. Sure, she wants something from you, but she's there because she elected to be there. She wasn't dragged kicking and screaming. You didn't barge in on her favorite TV show. She agreed to listen to you.

Even better, she's answering questions about herself and her family. You are using the data she provides to guide her through a marketing process, almost like painting by numbers, putting everything in place to get a better, more complete picture of your target consumer – and even figuring out if, in fact, she is your target consumer.

By giving her good reasons and incentives, she's registering for your sweepstakes – the "Magic Moment" – and even referring friends she thinks might want to hear about your product which will allow you to capture more data. Attracting even more people is a bonus. Your target is telling friends, creating viral marketing and generating repeat visits. In short, you have achieved your objective. You have converted an anonymous consumer and brought her into a data-driven relationship. Are you in a marketing fantasy, or what? No. It's real.

Best Practice:

Keep it simple. Just because you can do complex things doesn't mean you should; nor will it necessarily endear you to the consumer.

How many commercials have you watched that were entertaining and made you laugh and you even told your friends about? Plenty, I'll bet. Now, do you remember what was being advertised? Did you rush right out and buy it? You had a 30-second relationship with whatever was being advertised. Maybe you'll buy it next time you're out, but might you not give that brand a better shot if you'd had a non-intrusive five-minute dialogue with its sweepstakes or game page? And what if the game experience was so compelling that you visited seven times?

CASE STUDY

Westin Hotels "Experience Renewal" Promotion

Promotion overview and objectives
Westin wanted to educate consumers about their Renewal Suite and maximize the value of television's "The Apprentice: Martha Stewart." To accomplish this, a promotion was devised that would allow participants in a game to design their own renewal suite and enter a sweepstakes.

How it worked
Registrants were able to "drag and drop" design elements into a room to create the Ultimate Renewal Suite. The most creative designs were featured at a micro-Web site gallery. The Grand Prize winner received a trip for two to view the season finale of "The Apprentice: Martha Stewart" in New York with accommodations for six days and five nights in an Ultimate Renewal Suite at the Westin Times Square Hotel.

Key results
The contest generated an unheard-of average 11-minute stay and 6.5 visits per person. This was an incredible example of brand immersion. Would the company have done better through some other media channel? Think of all those people leaning forward, receptive, engaged in a truly interactive experience, immersed in the brand. This is clearly not the passive advertising of the past.

Best Practice:

Provide incentives for tell-a-friend (TAF) exchanges to drive the highest level of viral communication. The incentive will exponentially drive more viral activity.

A little respect, please

After screaming and complaining about traditional advertising throughout this book, you'd think we'd be finished by now. Well, not quite. Fact is, there are plenty of good things to be said about traditional advertising, not the least of which is that if it had not existed we would not appreciate interactive promotions as much as we do.

Okay, enough with the cynicism. Traditional advertising and marketing approaches have been invaluable in the development of Internet promotions. They have been the foundation upon which more defined, directed and successful campaigns have been built. But Elvis has left the building.

For the longest time, traditional advertising was all we had. There was no Internet, no technology that could blow open our eyes or minds. Now the technology is here and the marketing imagination is making use of it, the landscape has changed. Yet, the smart money says don't walk away from traditional marketing altogether. Instead, use it to support, feed and complement interactive promotions.

We can honestly say that as much as we cheer Internet marketing, traditional marketing gives it a real boost when the two are effectively linked together. The most successful campaigns successfully use traditional media not to sell the product, but to drive awareness and spur excitement. The 30-second spot then drives the 5-minute Web experience which drives frequency which really drives sales.

Best Practice:

Integrate a number of media channels to complement each other for best results.

One of the most telling signs of the durability of traditional advertising is the interest Yahoo, Google and eBay have taken in it. These online giants have recently made mega-dollar deals and investments in developing offline ad buying systems. Proof enough that traditional advertising is not going away. But that doesn't mean its role won't change.

The evidence of successful traditional-Internet partnerships is plentiful. Look at one company you're very familiar with: Coca-Cola.

CASE STUDY

Coca-Cola's My Coke Rewards Loyalty Program

Promotion overview and objectives
The My Coke Rewards promotion was a consumer rewards program covering Coca-Cola's entire brand portfolio. It was the biggest promotion of any kind in their history. It even included a Spanish-language version that marks Coke's first genuinely bilingual, Internet-based initiative.

How it worked
The promotion, extending from February, 2006 to January, 2007 debuted in conjunction with the NCAA March Madness and the Academy Awards. My Coke Rewards was a dynamically-driven, web-based program tailored to the individual consumer. The program debuted on 20-ounce containers where consumers found under-the-cap codes on Coca-Cola products including Coca-Cola Classic, Diet Coke and Coca-Cola Zero. The codes were entered for instant wins and points at MyCokeRewards.com where consumers created an account. Once an account was established the codes could also be entered through a mobile phone. Points could be redeemed for a variety of prizes displayed on the site. More than 4 billion codes were issued. People were directed to the site through any number of media channels including product packaging, point-of-sale materials, print and broadcast.

Key results

The results have been sparkling. While we cannot reveal exact statistics, let's just say everyone was very pleased with the length of the average consumer visit, the number of repeat visits per consumer, the average opt-in and tell-a-friend rates and the time of brand immersion per visitor. The statistics were also accurate – again, the big plus of measurability.

Weigh the cost of the promotion against the repeated exposure to the consumer and tell-a-friend referrals and see how that ROI fares against using traditional means exclusively. Yet, eliminating the traditional points of contact could severely compromise the potential success of similar promotions.

Other examples of old and new approaches abound. Southwest Airlines handed out eDecoders at high-traffic, major airports to drive consumers to their Web site to see if they'd won a prize. The eDecoders were coded game pieces which could only be decoded at the promotion Web site. While at the site, visitors were able to familiarize themselves with its features and capabilities enhancing the possibilities of future visits and Web usage. In addition, we were able to tell which airport the decoders were from, which helped analyze market demographics.

Baskin-Robbins worked the same type of promotion from the opposite end in a "print'n'win" approach. Its Web site visitors could print eDecoder game pieces with scrambled images from their computers. They were sent to the local Baskin-Robbins to unscramble them and see if they'd won ice cream. At the site they also registered for a chance-to-win a number of prizes as well as receive future offers from Baskin-Robbins.

Marketing today goes from online to offline and offline to online with surprising facility. It's easy. It's smooth. It works. You just have to know how.

What's really interesting throughout all these examples is the recognition that technology allows the creation of a one-on-one relationship. Traditionally, a store-keeper could do that, but that "closeness" couldn't scale high enough. That is no longer an issue. Personalized, relevant, two-way communication on a global scale has arrived and will be required to win in the New World of Marketing.

CHAPTER 8:

Shoring up the brand

As effective as interactive promotions can be, success is not automatic. Promotions of this kind are tools to be used appropriately, deliberately and with specific goals in mind. Certain promotions work better with certain products and there has to be a logical tie-in between the prizes awarded and the sponsoring brand for the connection to be effective.

Northwest Airlines isn't going to give away ice cream to attract the consumers it wants and Baskin-Robbins isn't going to award Frequent Flyer Miles to draw its target market. Those aren't the audiences each brand wants to attract. However, the right promotion combined with the right prizes will attract the audience you're seeking.

Best Practice:

Don't forget the brand. It must be part of the interactive experience. Even if you've created something fun and engaging, if the brand message isn't incorporated, you've failed. Every marketing effort is a brand touch point that can either reinforce or harm a brand's equity. Keep this in mind in every aspect of the promotion.

In one of its first interactive promotions, Northwest Airlines invited WorldPerks mileage program members to play an online golf game. Golf made sense as a draw for WorldPerks members. Winners received travel- and golf-related prizes. In turn, they registered to participate (the Magic Moment!) and opted in for future communications from Northwest. The promotion connected with the right consumers. It presented something of interest to them and, in turn, consumers were willing to listen and participate. Response was better than expected. High enough, in fact, to keep Northwest busy with subsequent promotions.

CASE STUDY

Northwest Airlines WorldPerks® Wide World of Partners Promotion

Promotion overview and objectives

Northwest Airlines wanted to primarily make its customers aware of, and enhance their relationships with, the airline's mileage partners. It also wanted to strengthen its WorldPerks loyalty program and attract customers to the airline's vacation destinations. A "shuffle and play" logo-matching game was created that allowed participants to win valuable instant prizes – all products or services available from the airline's partners. Participants were also entered for a grand prize of a seven-night cruise.

How it worked

Visitors registered to play at the Northwest Airlines Web site. Their registration put them into the sweepstakes. They were then moved to another survey screen where they were asked WorldPerks-related questions and given the chance to opt-in to a series of informative and special offer emails from Northwest Airlines and its partners. From there, they went on to the game board which was a series of squares. In each square was a Northwest Airlines logo or the logo of one of its partners. When the game started, the squares traveled across the board. When the game ended, one logo was in the "Winner's Square." If that logo matched the participant's pre-selected logo, the entrant was a winner and received an instant prize. Entrants could play once a day.

Key results

The Northwest promotion was a good example of tuning in to your market. In that case, the promotion supported the company's loyalty program – WorldPerks – as much as it did the company.

This is where online promotions can be particularly effective: In developing and supporting brand loyalty programs, highly fertile ground for growth.

Research has repeatedly shown the value of loyalty programs for airlines, credit card companies, hospitality groups, retailers and almost every other marketing category:

- 94% of high-income households said their membership in a loyalty, rewards or frequent customer program had a strong to moderate influence on their purchasing decisions, versus 78% of all consumers
- 40% of loyalty program members referred at least one person to a program, while 21% referred four or more people to a program
- In high-income households, 90% of members referred one or more people to the program while 64% referred four or more people

Effective online promotions provide opportunities to maintain established brand relationships and nurture new ones. Through opt-in programs directed to receptive consumers, the promotions can:

- Lead to brand loyalty and create brand advocates
- Increase frequency of purchase and maximize lifetime value of a customer
- Attract new customers who might not otherwise purchase the brand
- Establish preference and value
- Target specific groups via promotional appeal
- Act as a long-term program identified with brands
- Cross-sell other brands
- Continue the permission-based approach
- Continue to deepen the relationship

While all these objectives may apply across the board with all consumers, building a loyalty program works to "capture" consumers and keep them from wandering away. It also rewards loyalists. Palm did exactly that recently with a special promotion.

CASE STUDY

Palm Pays Back Loyalty Promotion

Promotion overview and objectives

Palm was being outgunned by the big computer boys and decided it had to somehow fight back to hold its place in the market. They needed to make consumers aware of their products, boost their sales and build current – and future – customer loyalty. Palm devised a promotion, "Palm Pays Back," asking loyal customers to refer friends and family to the company and rewarding the loyalists generously with Palm Bucks (to be used for product purchases) for every referral that bought something.

How it worked

Palm customers were given the opportunity to register and send Palm-prepared emails to friends. The emails presented information about Palm's latest line of PDAs. For each email sent, the customer received Palm Bucks, and if the friend purchased a Palm product, even more Palm Bucks were awarded.

Key results

Not only was the promotion good for the loyalists, it was great for Palm as one in every five referrals bought a Palm product – a 20% response. And, of course, the new customers introduced to an array of products. Everybody won, hands down.

Again, it's the dynamic personalization the Internet allows that makes it a relevant choice for carrying messages for consumers. That's especially true for loyalty programs where "Dear Anonymous" has no place and "Dear Ms. Linda Connors, I have a special offer just for you works wonders."

CHAPTER 9:

Mom and Pops of the world, rejoice!

So far, everything we've said about interactive marketing appears to apply only to major corporations. After all, how could a small dry cleaning or car wash chain do what Coca-Cola or Dell does?

Conventional thinking tells you that Marie's Bridal Shop and the local three-outlet flower shop just don't have the wherewithal to create complex interactive Web sites replete with all the bells and whistles that a sophisticated sweepstakes or promotion requires. Small companies that operate in a galaxy not even close to the Fortune 500, the onesies and twosies and the "mom & pop" shops that are really the backbone of commerce in our country, are often advised to reach their audience through direct mail coupon packets addressed "Occupant," newspaper ads and inserts, local radio and, perhaps, cable television. That's the way to go, yessiree.

But, as the character Sportin' Life in "Porgy and Bess" says, 'it ain't necessarily so.'

After all, wouldn't that one-store clothing boutique love to be able to do what Target or Macy's does? This is an equal opportunity nation and small companies need to have – ought to have – similar opportunities as the big guys do.

And there are a lot of little guys out there. Of the 24 million taxed businesses in the United States, 20 million of them have modest revenues ranging from $100K to $250K. Together that adds up to real money.

However, as many small businesses as there are, they still can't pretend to be or spend as though they are mega-companies. While there are reams of data showing that promotions work, they are still complex, expensive and can be risky.

Small businesses are frustrated in attempting online promotions. That's because of factors we call "massive friction" that translate into costs they can't afford. These include:

- Technology and software requirements
- Prize costs and fulfillment logistics
- Legal compliance and costs
- Time consumption
- Overall expense

These factors are just too much for small business owners to deal with and remain profitable. For all those reasons, small businesses have justifiably stayed away from online interactive promotions. They can't undertake the expensive ventures.

Now there's good news for them: technology is democratizing the tools and content management apparatus needed for creating, maintaining and supporting online interactive marketing. You can see that everyday with the proliferation of Internet blogs and Web site such as YouTube and MySpace and plenty of other additions from the time of this publication and the time you read this book

The little guys have seen what online interactive promotions can do and now they have their shot at the big time. That's because new software applications have been generated in recognition of the vast potential small business marketing represents.

For example, at ePrize we've developed a program to specifically address the needs of small businesses of all kinds. We call it Caffeine (www.caffeinenow.com) and it works to enhance the marketing power of companies with small markets or local niches.

Caffeine operates using key elements:

- Wizard-driven, fully automated promotion building tools
- Pooled Drawings™ to leverage existing prize pools to save time and money
- Pay only for performance

The value to small businesses is obvious. They get the same plusses for their interactive efforts as the big guys:

- The initiation and nurturing of one-to-one relationships
- Improved overall advertising response rates
- Cutting through the ad clutter and having a message stand out
- Converting "browsers" or "shoppers" into registered users and customers
- Driving reach, frequency and sales
- Enhancing their "brand" value and recognition
- A level playing field with the big brands.

All at a realistic, affordable cost. Again, thank you, technology.

In addition, local companies can now go national and even international with Web-based promotions. Netflix and Amazon operate out of warehouses and offices in a few locations, yet their audiences are spread out all over. Aunt Millie's Homemade Salad Dressings can now run an online promotion on a national scale to a smaller audience that has previously been untapped, but is receptive to the message and throw in an incentive to ensure the consideration.

Small businesses, which are, in effect, niche marketers reaching a small audience interested in their products and services, gain far more than they could with traditional marketing methods. And consumers receive the prize opportunities provided by a promotion or sweepstakes as well as learning about a small business they may have never considered before. In the end, it's a real chance for a long-lasting, one-on-one relationship, the kind that has sustained businesses of all sizes and will continue to do so in the future.

Those small businesses that dismiss such an opportunity are falling into the same danger zone as are big companies that don't see what is here today and tomorrow is bringing. And small companies are usually much more vulnerable than the big guys.

CHAPTER 10:

The rules of engagement

This is about interactive integrity. Forget that and you can forget success.

We've talked a lot about the opportunities marketers have with interactive selling, especially any form of it that includes promotion through the Internet. These are no longer the days of direct mail going into the waste basket or unwanted telephone solicitors being dismissed with a hang-up of the call. Those are ultimately harmless intrusions a consumer can ignore. Technology has made incredible inroads into people's privacy; spam, computer tracking, even legitimate email communications allow more entry than ever into the consumer's personal life. So, along with such opportunities comes the responsibility of respecting the consumer.

It's important to underscore, once again, that the essential elements of the one-on-one relationship are relevance and trust. Both are critical to building the relationship and missing either can wound even the largest of brands.

First is the issue of relevance. If a promotion or message matters to the consumer, he or she may listen and perhaps take the action the marketer desires. A promotion has to mean something to the individual targeted otherwise there will be no connection established, no chance for a brand relationship. The product – and promotion – have to be directed to an audience that cares, and the audience will only care if the promotion is relevant to them.

For example, a "Win-a-trip-to-Paris" sweepstakes or a promotion offering concert tickets or exclusive downloads for music enthusiasts will probably have relatively broad market appeal and be relevant incentives for a great number of people. But if you're going to market dog food, you'd probably prefer to target those people who buy dog food, i.e., dog owners, pet stores, kennels, etc. – people who are interested in what is happening in the world of dog food. So, you do your best to reach those people because your product is relevant to their needs. It makes sense to create a meaningful promotion that somehow involves dogs or dog food *and* reaches the people most likely to grow into a brand-loyal relationship with you. Granted, there will always be a few people for whom participating in a promotion, regardless of what is, is its own end. For the most part, however, cat owners aren't going to be attracted to a dog food promotion. It's irrelevant to them.

Yet, even if the promotion is relevant and meaningful, ultimately the consumer must trust the marketer.

The trust comes in two ways. The first, that the marketer will deliver on what is promised – a great product that lives up to expectations as well as the reward offered in the promotion.

The second form of trust is just as, or even more, important. It's all about privacy and the information the consumer provides. Because to enter the sweepstakes or promotion, the consumer must exchange information and the question arises: I am giving up some privacy here. How will the marketer treat that information? Will it be shared? Sold? If so, to whom? Will it be abused? Protected? How ethical is the promoter? This is where trust and integrity are interlocked.

Some consumers – albeit few – aren't concerned about what is done with their information. Maybe that's because they genuinely don't care, aren't aware of the possible implications or, in some cases, provide false data (even though that may compromise their chances of winning) that carries no consequences for them.

The majority of consumers, however, do care quite a bit about the information they hand over even if they agree to do so as an entry fee to a promotion. They've chosen to opt-in and generally want to know how their data will be used.

That's where you come in and, in order to succeed initially and in the long run, have to play by the rules. Given the lightning fast nature of today's communication technology, if you don't play it straight, the word gets out and you won't be playing for long.

Advertisements must be transparent, allow consumers to opt-in and provide value – an exchange. But don't overstep the bounds. Sell the consumer's phone number for text messaging and you may lose the customer forever.

Best Practice:

When asking people to opt-in, clearly tell them what you're asking for and how it will be used.

Trust-based, permissive methods of communicating in a personalized way on a global scale are the surest techniques for gaining access to the eye, ear and debit card of today's consumer. Provide value in your message and you're not intruding; you're informing, investing and increasing the loyalty of once-dubious consumers who have finally found a brand they can trust.

In my opinion, in order to earn the trust and respect of the consumer – no matter how they play the game – there are certain things an ethical marketer must do.

First of all, consider the legal aspects of your promotion. There are plenty. We can't cover them all here, but enough to point out the general issues you need to address.

It seems so obvious, but if you promise something, you must deliver it. If the sweepstakes first prize is a trip to Paris, there must be a winner that receives a trip to Paris. If you're promising coupons or discounts or rebates or game tickets or downloads, you must provide them. It would seem that this would go without saying, but there are unscrupulous marketers who simply don't do what they say, or provide X when Y has been promised.

Sometimes the failure to live up to a promise is unintentional. Someone drops the ball and forgets to distribute a prize or it gets lost along the way. That is no excuse. All the consumer knows is that you didn't come through. Fix it quickly or kiss your chances of a relationship with the consumer goodby and if, indeed, there was something shady going on, say "hello," instead, to the authorities. They will soon be knocking at your door.

Beyond that, there are more sweepstakes and promotions rules and regulations than you sometimes can imagine. They vary from state to state and are complemented by federal trade statutes. Think of all the fine print and weasel-type disclaimers on sweepstakes entry forms and coupons. Comprehensive and complex? You bet. But they're there for a reason and compliance is absolute. Try to abbreviate or sidestep them and suddenly you'll receive an unwanted inquiry from a governmental agency. But why would you want to sidestep them in any case? Your whole purpose is to earn the trust of the consumer. You do that by playing it straight.

Putting aside the legalities needed to run a promotion, comes the matter of the information you gather, your "privacy policy" if you will. Make no mistake, this is critical.

Privacy, in our country, has always been perceived as a basic right. The issue of privacy in a variety of forms has frequently made it into the courts – all the way to the Supreme Court in some instances.

Bottom line for marketers is this: Post your privacy policy in clear terms and stick to it. Let people know how you intend to use their information – keeping it private, sharing it with affiliates, selling it outright to other marketers – and let them make the choice of whether to opt-in or opt-out. Luring consumers in with unclear privacy provisions ultimately doesn't work. If they learn you've misled them (even if unintentionally), the resentment will come in the form of a backlash. And, frankly, what's the point of bringing in people who, if they understood the policy, wouldn't be there? There's not much to gain from them. Better to be clear and be receptive to the people who choose to participate. No matter how small that niche may seem to you when compared to the mass market, they're the ones who may be willing to enter into a rewarding one-on-one relationship with you and they're the ones who will be willing to listen to your message.

Best Practice:

When your privacy policy changes, let people know either by email (if they're opted-in) or with an announcement on your Web site.

What the real issue is, of course, is control of information. The consumer wants to be in charge of the data. I'll tell you just about anything about me if I know I control the flow of that information. The fear is the information will fall into the wrong hands, everything from unwanted marketers to hackers to governmental agencies to identity theft scammers. More than that, however, is the fundamental concept that the consumer wants to call the shots.

The reality is that few of us have that control over data. Once it's on a Web site there is no 100% certainty that it will remain confidential. But that isn't necessarily the point. The point is people want to believe they really are in charge of the relationship with the marketer and therefore are in charge of the information they pass along. It's the perception that's important.

Your task, in order to be successful here, is to ensure trust and confidence in your privacy policy even though you have the right to change it at any time (which would be a good thing to point out in the policy) and that the policy is not really a contract with the consumer. It's the concept of "goodwill" and it can take you a long way toward earning the trust of the consumer.

For evidence of the privacy concerns of consumers, take a look at what recently happened with Facebook, a popular social networking site primarily aimed at high school and college students. Facebook debuted a feature called "News Feeds" that presented a compilation of everything members do on the site. This included adding and deleting friends, new interests, relationship changes, all things that would be displayed on the individual members' pages anyway. The new feature did it automatically and presented it without being asked.

Facebook users were not happy – and that is an understatement – with the company's move. The information is there for viewing anyhow, right? What's the big deal? thought Facebook. The big deal is that members did not have control over their information. Facebook was using it in a way that was unintended by the members. Facebook thought they were doing their users a favor, making things easier and fresh. Members didn't see it quite that way. They saw their information being distributed in ways they hadn't expected. It was a jarring realization that they weren't in control of their data.

Facebook was legally within its rights, but so what? Did they really want to turn off their members? Hardly. Lesson learned: Consumers want to be in charge, even if they really aren't.

In the long term, there's more to gain by honoring that delusion and making it a reality than by taking advantage of it.

The bottom line on the subject is simple: As an industry, we have to forcefully self-regulate to prevent outside interests from getting into our business. We also have to provide outrageous value to consumers in order to overcome their privacy concerns. Yet, even if we do that, we cannot abuse the privilege we've been given. To do so compromises your brand and ultimately defeats all your marketing efforts.

CHAPTER 11:

Protecting the Golden Goose

As in every commercial enterprise, when someone succeeds, everyone else wants in.   When that happens, things can go whacky and that can shake out the field and hurt everyone. In interactive promotional marketing that includes consumers and marketers.   How then do we protect the "Golden Goose" from threats or exploitation that could eliminate the flow of golden eggs?

In two words, we can't. The Golden Goose could easily fly away because of abuses or legitimate competition. But you can protect your own credibility.

The abuses could come from unsavory or don't-have-a-clue marketers who intentionally or naively exploit the consumer's trust and don't deliver on what is promised, or take the short-term route and distribute information the consumer has provided for their own gain and not for the prospective customer. The public distrust of interactive dialogue created will hurt credibility across the board and everyone suffers.

If that happens, our industry will come under the watchful eye of state and federal regulating agencies and free competition will be compromised. We don't need those kinds of headlines.   Our responsibility as legitimate, conscientious marketers is to self-regulate to avoid that governmental abyss as well as a scathing backlash from consumers.

However, we have to accept that possibility. Human nature being what it is, undoubtedly there are villains waiting to take advantage of the opportunities interactive online marketing present. There are plenty of bad guys out there who just don't care. Legitimate marketers cannot even entertain such activities or they can say "adios" to brand image. Would Coca-Cola, Southwest Airlines, the Gap or any other quality brand consider for even a nanosecond of taking advantage of the consumer? We think not.

Where the real threat to our Golden Goose lies is in over-saturation by online marketers and the ensuing tuning out, lack of interest and boredom on the part of consumers. But that threat is no different than a threat to and from any form of marketing. Smart marketers will survive. That's a Darwinian reality and, as is happening right now throughout the advertising community, the strong and smart are surviving, doing very well, thank you; they are adapting and coming out better for it. The weak, those who fail to adapt, well, chances are excellent they will go the route of the dodo bird.

Survival in this industry will call for constant innovation and improvement of online promotions. It will call for development and application of new technologies. It will also call for the recognition and addressing of global marketing and reaching out around the world for new markets in emerging economies or to sustain existing markets in mature economies.

That constant innovation and adaptation also applies to our understanding of the audiences we are talking to. Multi-culturalism is, in one form or another, almost continuously top-of-mind. Web sites cannot talk to their audiences with one voice. Not everyone speaks English. Not everyone lives in the U.S. Not everyone makes $1 million a year. Not everyone has the same hobbies or political or religious bent. But, and this is a big "but," all those differences are what ensure the success of interactive marketing, because the technology allows the development of specific programs, responses and formats for different groups in a cost-effective manner. It's called niche marketing and it applies not only to the narrow product being marketed but also to the narrow market being addressed.

As we move globally, this becomes a bigger concern. Check out a domestic example. Today, in the U.S., Spanish-language Web sites are commonplace. However, you can't simply translate English into Spanish and expect the same response you'd get in English. Along with the language translation there needs to be a cultural adjustment; a different tonality and approach; in other words, a sensitivity to another culture. We think of it as cultural authenticity – a consideration for and acceptance of distinct mores, values and tenets.

In the same vein, you can't take a game or promotion that works in the U.S and simply plop it into France or South Africa or Japan by translating it into the national language. It doesn't work that way. Failing to consider the nuances of cultural differences will ensure failure of your message. But again, the beauty of the Internet is that differences are easy to address and transcend as long as you actually do it.

Best Practice:

Use IPP/dynamic content to segment and refine your prospects and to deliver relevant messages to them.

The actual survival of the Golden Goose is not really the issue. What is the issue is who will benefit from the Golden Goose's golden eggs. That reward will go to whomever is hungrier, more tuned in to the consumer and more willing to respond to the consumer's desires with smart and relevant marketing. That's because the Golden Goose is not the process or the bounty. The Golden Goose *is* the consumer, and the consumer will follow the marketer that respects him and gives him what he thinks he needs. Darwin would be loving that.

CHAPTER 12:

Where we are now

W e're all over the place. Ten years ago, we had no idea we'd be where we are today. Those who say they knew are kidding themselves. And as advanced as we think we are, we're clearly at the very embryonic stage of interactive promotional marketing. There are hints of what's to come, but first we have to deal with what is.

What we see is mass marketing as we know it making its way to the exit and, instead, marketers gathering data and working to establish individual relationships with consumers.

They're doing it through brand immersive games of all kinds that have forever changed the way marketers view the consumer. Progressive marketers are zeroing in on the concept of promotion programs that are custom designed for their particular needs. This is done through proprietary software and a spectacularly innovative interactive promotion platform that enables a brand marketer to gather specific data and purchase patterns for specific consumers not only from a current campaign, but also from every future promotion in which that same consumer participates.

With individuals visiting multiple promotions in some cases up to 12 times, the platform allows a marketer to ask different questions each visit and drill down into the individual's preferences and background. (It's like dating, remember?) Gathering different, more detailed information each time to allow the marketer to enhance the "knowledge" experience. And that, too, will undoubtedly change. The only question is when.

Technology, in fact, is changing our marketing culture so quickly that the only thing we can be sure of is change. Still, there are some developments that have emerged and shown some staying power. At the risk of being redundant, let's take a look at where we are these days.

Driving consumers to the Internet to participate in pro-motions has rapidly surfaced as one of the most powerful tac-tics for pinpointing individual consumer's demographics and preferences. This is how we see things shaping up:

1. The centerpiece channel

Interactive promotions have become the glue that holds together the larger marketing message. When campaigns run in multiple channels, those media direct consumers to an online interactive promotion that becomes the focal point where information can be gathered on visitors so they can be further engaged. The Gap used in-store promotions, a TV campaign and a major-city tour to invite consumers to submit pictures of themselves wearing Gap clothing their own way to an online site with a chance- to-win a gift card and a trip. Keep in mind, too, PepsiOne launched without a TV component. Are you getting nervous yet?

2. Intelligent promotions

Thanks to IPP and dynamically driven content, brands can interact with consumers in a true one-on-one fashion to per-sonalize the experience. Sites using IPP ask those who log in to answer a few questions. The consumer's responses deter-mine the very next screen she sees. Thereafter, the ask-answer process continues throughout the visit and everything an individual consumer sees on the site is dynamically gener-ated based on that individual's previous responses and gath-ered information. Different visitors will have a different game experience and receive different coupons, different special offers. The site responds in "intelligent" fashion to the inter-ests and experiences of the *individual* visitor. By generating offers and information relevant to the interests of the individ-ual, the brand is laying down the foundation upon which a potential long-term relationship can be built. In short, IPP and the concept of dynamic content and the relevance it offers hold the key to capturing the consumer's interest and ultimate loyalty.

CASE STUDY

7-Eleven Pizza and a Movie Summer Promotion

Promotion overview and objectives

7-Eleven wanted to attract Web site visitors and gain opt-ins through a game-driven instant-win promotion. An "X-Men: The Last Stand" movie-themed promotion was devised whereby registrants could play to win a range of instant prizes based around the movie as well as four grand prizes (non-instant) of trips for two to a 20th Century Fox movie set. Prizes were male-skewed in anticipation of a heavier male participation rate.

How it worked

Participants registered and were asked various demographic questions and given a choice as to the video game format they preferred to play. They were then directed to the appropriate game page. After playing, the registrant would learn whether he or she had won a prize. If not, a consolation coupon (this is where the pizza comes in) was offered. Participants were also given the opportunity to tell-a-friend. This was supported with a "you win, I win" incentive, meaning that if the friend won in the game, the participant would, too. Along with the tell-a-friend channel, the promotion was supported with in-store displays at 7-Eleven shops. At the end of the game experience, participants were given a link to the 7-Eleven corporate Web site.

Key results

The promotion received a positive response from a number of demographic groups with the strongest being women over the age of 25. The demographic findings gave 7-Eleven insight into who to market to and how to better use the various media channels to reach their target audience. In all, women made up 64% of the respondents. It was also found registrants re-played the instant win game 5.6 times during the promotion at an average of 3 minutes per visit for a total of over 16 minutes of immersion in the 7-Eleven brand. In addition, the viral aspect of the program, the tell-a-friend referrals, were the biggest reason people found out about the promotion.

3. Customer- and channel-specific promotions

Online promotions are now reaching businesses and employees as well as consumers. Fedex used an interactive promotion to target companies that ship to Japan. LG Electronics used the same approach to encourage the sales staffs of retail stores to recommend LG products to customers. The promotions can be shaped to the particular customer (business or individual) in the channel the client seeks to influence.

4. Low-cost, points-based rewards

Interactive promotions make developing and executing point-based consumer reward loyalty programs easier and more cost-effective than other mediums such as direct mail. The online option offers marketers a chance to have more one-on-one interactions with its consumers while giving consumers the ability to enter into these relationships on their own terms. Programs for Pampers, Disney, Palm and Coca-Cola have increased dialogue with consumers while building brand loyalty through an easy, comfortable online channel.

5. SMS/Mobile marketing

Mobile marketing now often means communicating with wireless-phone customers through text messaging. SMS can be linked with interactive promotions to gain consumer feedback. Conference attendees, for example, can be asked to text-message information about themselves to a number to find out if they are a prize winner, to give reactions to products or both. SMS can also be used for sweepstakes and contests. A recent promotion by Kodak, The Kong-Sized Smiles Sweepstakes, invited participants to enter a photo of a giant smile for a chance-to-win the grand prize of a VIP trip to New York. Participants were encouraged to enter the sweepstake via their camera phone, via SMS. The promotion was successful.

6. Internationalization

Increasingly, multi-national corporations are extending their promotions around the world. Coca-Cola and Motorola have been using online games and prizes to promote products in Asia, Europe, Canada, Mexico, and other regions to maximize reach and impact. The trend is to leverage an investment in a domestic promotion by adapting the campaign to reach multiple markets. But, as noted, in order to have chance of success, there must be cultural authenticity.

7. Consumer insight over time

The true gold in marketing is a brand's ability to gather increasing amounts of information about individual consumers over time and use it to create win-win situations. Savvy marketers are turning to interactive promotions. Today's technology allows a marketer to recognize a repeat visitor and use that opportunity to learn more about the consumer. Over time the brand is able to build a very rich profile of each consumer. Interactive promotions encourage a consumer to return numerous times to earn additional chances for a prize or other rewards. With this capability, marketers can develop a strategic calendar plan to reach specific users at various times of the year with seasonal rewards, offers or tips or to contact a variety of audiences, each of which may be most receptive at a particular point on the calendar.

And speaking of calendars, we should also point out the concept of "Tent Pole Strategy" – an approach that can be put to good use in interactive promotions.

Tent Pole Strategy originated with television where it involved concentrating a brand's most intense marketing efforts around programs in specific time periods. The goal was to keep consumers loyal during "in between" or lower marketed time slots. This is still a common approach for the TV networks. They use one or two "big-time" shows to anchor each night and complete the evening with smaller, lower-cost gap fillers.

This also applies to interactive marketers. For example, Coca-Cola will follow the calendar to create its series of promotions: an NCAA Basketball promotion in the spring, a summer promotion of some sort, a fall football promotion and an end-of-year holiday promotion. The promotions are scheduled just often enough to keep consumers aware of Coca-Cola even with a lull between major promotions. The scheduling is similar to the radio and television media buys that use flights of 2-3 weeks of heavy advertising frequency then go off-air for a period of time before the next flight. In the consumer's mind, the advertising flight is still on.

With this strategy, scheduled "pillar" promotions hold up the "tent" to keep the consumer aware of the brand.

8. Driving frequency

Today's promotions not only drive reach and attention, but frequency as well. For example, consumers may receive an on-screen trading card. When they collect the entire set – by repeat visits to the site – they win the grand prize. Marketers can reach consumers once through an online promotion and enjoy them returning voluntarily 5 or 10 times more.

CASE STUDY

Citibank "collect and win" Look Who's Banking Online With Citibank Promotion

Promotion overview and objective

Citibank had several objectives in mind with this promotion. They wanted to

_ *teach customers how to navigate through their Web site,*
_ *demonstrate the ease and convenience of banking online and*
_ *build loyalty and expose customers to online CRM programs. A "Look Who's Banking Online With Citibank" scavenger hunt game was created in which participants collected game pieces by answering trivia questions. Collecting all the game pieces (12) made you eligible to win a grand prize – one of three "trips of a lifetime." "Instant win" opportunities would also be available throughout the game.*

How it worked

The landing page had separate sign-ins for Citibank customers and non-customers. Non-customers went to a registration page where their contact information was entered and they were offered the chance to opt-in for future information emails. Customers signed in using their regular user name and password. Once registered, participants were given the details and the game began. Each entrant was given three trivia questions per visit. Each time they answered a question correctly, they received a game piece. Each piece represented a different person who banks online at Citibank. Once a participant collected all 12 pieces, they won. Registrants could also click the lower menu bar to play for instant wins including laptops, portable DVD players, digital cameras, Apple iPods and more..

Key results

On average, each entrant played the Citibank promotion an amazing 23.7 times and spent approximately 5 minutes on each visit for a total of about 118.6 minutes spent with the brands showing that trivia is not trivial.

9. Rich media

The term "rich media" refers to a broad range of digital interactive media. Rich media can be downloadable or may be embedded in a Web page. If downloadable, it can be viewed or used offline with media players such as Real Network's RealPlayer, Microsoft Media Player or Apple's QuickTime, among others. The defining characteristic of rich media is that it exhibits dynamic motion. This motion may occur over time or in direct response to user interaction. Two examples of dynamic motion that occur over time are a streaming video newscast and a stock ticker that continually updates itself. An example of dynamic motion in response to user interaction is a pre-recorded Web cast coupled with a synchronized slide show that allows user control. Another is an animated, interaction presentation file embedded in a Web page.

While banner ads have become passé and pop-ups a nuisance, the use of so-called rich media ads is poised for rapid growth, industry experts say. Rich media combines animation, video and sound with interactive features. What's more, rich media can deliver instant detailed feedback ranging from how many seconds PC users spend viewing an ad to what they click to next. It could entice users to submit demographic data in real time by filling out a form, or even make an online purchase. A recent survey by DoubleClick, which distributes online ads, found rich media generates substantially greater brand recognition and higher sales activity than static online ads. Look for expanded rich media use in adver-gaming. The proliferation of broadband connections allows for running a digitized TV spot while a game is loading or carrying out an interactive experience within the confines of a banner ad on the company's site. Games such as NASCAR racing, can incorporate company logos in the background and branded vehicles or gear.

10. Digital rewards

No longer do we need to sort through mail, enter data and send back a check or coupon. With interactive promotions, the consumer enters the data and can instantly receive a digital reward online. A gift code for amazon.com can be used immediately to make a purchase – and Amazon handles the fulfillment. The interactive approach is less expensive and more efficient than conventional means while providing more accurate data collection. It also gives the consumer immediate gratification which is what most purchases are all about.

With immediate returns on investment and highly measurable, significant cost savings, interactive promotions have transformed the way brands interact with consumers.

And with things moving as quickly as they are, companies that either ignore the marketing dynamics around them or choose not to act on them, can start selling off their assets right now – while they're still worth something.

CHAPTER 13:

Key moves to make in Interactive marketing

L ike lists? This is a valuable one, worth the price of admission. Keep these "best practices" in mind as you develop your interactive promotions and you'll optimize your chances for success. While we list 25 critical points here, you'll discover many more along the way – best practices that apply to you.

1. Don't ask the consumer the same question twice. Get the data the first time.
2. If you do ask a question, act on the answer. Consumers are irritated if you ask and then act as if you didn't.
3. Gather information over time, across promotions and aggregate. That's a key reason you're doing the promotion in the first place.
4. Make it fun. Fun always works better than not fun.
5. Minimize clicks for your promotion. Fewer clicks mean less drop-off.
6. Don't make it too complicated. Just because you can do something technologically cool, doesn't mean you should. Consumers may find it isn't worth the trouble to hang in.
7. Know your targets and what interests them. That's the Value Exchange. Keep the promotion relevant to the audience you want to attract.
8. Avoid "one size fits all" marketing. Use dynamic content (IPP) to connect one-to-one.
9. Clearly define what you want to say and create communication priorities. If you say too much, you say nothing at all.
10 Don't just do what everyone else is doing just because everyone is doing it. You're not a lemming. Ask yourself: Does it work for my objective? Does it fit my brand?
11. Experiment, always evolve. You don't know if you don't try.
12. Kaizen Evolutionary concepts (continual improvement) are just as important as revolutionary concepts. Don't be afraid of baby steps (just don't stand still).

13. Make it a branding experience. Don't forget the brand. It's at the heart of the promotion.
14. Keep the tone, prizes and experience consistent with the brand. It's easy to get caught up in the promotion, but don't let it walk away from the brand identity.
15. Clearly identify your objective. Know where you want to go. And make sure the promotion will take you there.
16. Quantify your objective. Have your process in place and ready to digest your findings.
17. Measure results. You can and you should. The data is critical for future use.
18. Don't use Interactive media as a stand-alone marketing tool. Integrate it with other formats to achieve synergy and maximize results.
19. Develop a communication plan to target and drive the right people to your interactive campaign. They don't just show up.
20. Enable tell-a-friend/viral function. Make it easy for people who like your promotion to tell others, and give them incentive to tell.
21. But don't rely on "viral marketing" as your sole communication vehicle for interactive marketing. Buzz needs support.
22. Use Interactive marketing as an ongoing solution, not just as an in/out strategy. Incorporate it into your communications mix.
23. Interactive marketing is a multi-channel solution, not just business-to-consumer. Use it internally and for business-to-business.
24. Fail forward. In any medium, mistakes happen. Don't let them stop you; learn from them and grow. Have fun along the way.
25. And remember: Know the brand. Know your consumer. Understand your promotion and what you want to accomplish. The message will come through.

CHAPTER 14:

Where are we going?

Just as it was difficult 10 years ago to know where we'd be today, it's difficult today to say where we'll be tomorrow. However, some projections are likely.

We can say goodbye to conventional ad agencies and media buying companies and their advertising approaches as we knew them. Noted authorities in the field agree. As Christopher Vollmer, John Frelinghuysen and Randall Rothenberg point out in their article "The Future of Advertising is Now," *strategy+business*, (June, 2006), the signs are everywhere. The ways consumers receive their information have changed – forever.

Marketers will reach their customers in new and seemingly novel ways (for them, but not for the new generations), in ways referred to as "nonlinear and engagement-focused" media. Consumers will be exposed to brand messages through their wi-fi laptops and cell phones and devices yet uninvented.

The Jack Myers Media Business Report tells us magazines have been losing revenue to the Internet at the rate of about 2% per year since 1998, radio's been losing listeners and broadcast advertising revenues declined in both 2004 and 2005 – the first time they've ever decreased two years in a row. The third may be 2006 (confirming figures were unavailable at the time of publication).

The days of mass message spewing in hopes some of it sticks somewhere are fading. Instead, we'll see marketers adapting their messages to reach their niche audiences and consumers becoming involved with various brands through loyalty programs.

Marketers will also have to change their thinking about how they conduct interactive promotions. Loyalty campaigns won't necessarily have to take the form of a sweepstakes or a contest or a series of coupons. A variety of elements will be linked together through numerous media channels to create 360° of exposure – and the online channel will be the cornerstone of the communication effort. Adios television, sorry, you're no longer the star, but we still want you in a supporting role.

The idea of one-to-one interactive marketing instead of the one-to-many of mass marketing will grow in importance as smaller, more profitable markets are recognized and addressed while silly, expensive campaigns that may be highly memorable and fun – but fail to gather consumer data, meet objectives or boost sales for the brand – lose their glow. With that, we'll see a greater emphasis on outcomes, not inputs. The big question won't be whether we spend $45 million for our TV budget. It will be what will the $45 million produce? A question that can be answered by online metrics, but leaves an embarrassing silence and nervous coughing in the management suites on Madison Avenue.

Success will continue to be determined by the word-of-mouth of excited, engaged consumers touting a brand to their friends, as consumers always have. But it won't be because of a TV commercial or a print ad. The buzz will be generated by a multi-media sweepstakes, a contest, a download, a validation to the new generation that they – and the brands they favor – have arrived together in a new space, in a new time in a dramatically changing marketing world.

Look to that new generation to determine where we as marketers go next. Marketers should be working to gain permission to provide consumers with marketing messages. Yes, we are making bigger, Internet-ready screens for their cell phones and PDAs, but we can't think that just because the channel is there, we can return to our intrusive ways.

Research shows 42% of mobile customers are open to ads if they're relevant, if they asked for them, if they're free or if they'll get coupons or free services. Perhaps those mobile customers know that mobile advertisers are chomping at the bit to reach them. Research firm Yankee Group says U.S. mobile advertising was expected to go to $150 million from $45 million in 2005 ($274 billion was spent on all advertising in the U.S. in 2005) and could reach $2 billion by 2010. But unless those ads and messages are relevant to the consumer, the same backlash that tunes out traditional advertising will be directed at mobile ads. Today's young consumers know when a branding message is foisted upon them. More than ever, they will be able to tune out unwanted marketers with greater ease, determination and glee. We can't forget we live in a "what's-in-it-for-me?" society.

A consensus exists among online company executives that the advertising revenue potential of the Internet is underestimated. And ZenithOptimedia, a media and planning firm, reports this year the Internet will have more money spent on it than outdoor and soon will overtake radio.

Marketing communications must re-invent themselves to be more consumer-oriented than ever. Brand marketers who pay attention to the power of digital media, develop ways to communicate with their target markets, focus on metrics that accurately measure outcomes, create integrated multi-media campaigns and implement appealing interactive promotions will still be around to greet the next few decades.

It's these leading marketers, perceptive and astute, who are reading the tea leaves and taking them seriously. They're putting more money into digital media and taking it away from inefficient traditional media outlets.

As broadband penetration grows, more Internet entertainment options will be available making the marketing picture much more attractive to marketers who "get it" and much scarier for those who don't. It's bad times coming for those who insist on "pushing" until the end. The end is nearer than they think.

Consumer behavior is farther ahead than that of the marketers. In this period of transition, those marketers who stake their claim, take the risks and the initiative will be the ones to celebrate success. The marketing game is being re-invented and while the snake oil salesmen will always be there in one form or another, they will have fewer customers willing to buy.

Marketing has always been partly art, partly science; a psychological game of behavioral probabilities geared to produce certain results. There are no guarantees ever about outcomes, but marketing is now more science than it has ever been. However, it has not walked away from art.

Today, the culture of passion is meeting discipline. Creativity and accountability. Each in balance with the other to make the opportunities of this period in marketing measurable, accountable, creative and interactive. It is a grand time right now with a new era of creativity coming to life all around us. Together, these factors are sure to ignite innovation in marketing as well as in media and entertainment. It's all evolving at a faster-than-expected pace and turning things around. (Did you ever think the video games industry would be bigger than the movie industry? It is.)

The media is acknowledging the changes, sometimes grudgingly. Yet, they're acting on it. NBC is cutting programs and re-investing the estimated $750 million in savings in high-growth areas of media and expects digital revenue to top $1billion by 2008. The intent is to exploit technology and re-focus resources as they acknowledge their transformation into a digital media company. ABC News is creating a 15-minute newscast for the Web that is separate from its ABC World News. The networks are even producing podcasts. As Bob Dylan's song says, "the times, they are a changin'."

Even the world of academia is tuning in to the shift. Undergraduate and graduate degrees in Integrated Marketing Communications are being offered at a number of colleges and universities. Would they be making an investment in training the next generation in this field if it weren't viable? If they didn't see the demand?

If you want to synopsize the future of interactive marketing, here are the trends we see coming.

1. More opportunities for consumers to opt-out and avoid advertising.

   TIVO and satellite radio are just the start. The cat-and-mouse game between marketers and consumers will become more sophisticated.

2. Increased pressure to pay out on value exchange.

   If consumers can opt-out of communications more easily, value exchange pressure increases. Marketers must make opting-in more worthwhile.

3. Value-added content first, branding second.

   The reverse of traditional theory of "brand is hero." The brand, of course, will still be extremely important, but it can't exist on name alone.

4. Continued merging of technology and gear.

   Think how cell phones, PDAs, camera phones and MP3 players have merged into one device. The obvious big one is TV and computer combining to produce interactive television.

5. Greater accessibility to consumers.

   As consumers – and the world – become more wired, there are more ways to reach people at more times. As traditional windows of contact opportunities narrow (no more Big 3 TV networks), marketers will look for and find more ways to reach them. Benefits: Increased relevance at the time the message is delivered and less clutter in newer settings. But lack of clutter only lasts so long before all marketers converge.

6. Better measurement and accountability.
   Better tracking of consumers through the entire marketing mix/branding experience.
7. More virtual assets, experiences.
   Ultimately results in better branded content as marketers learn what appeals to consumers; also, prizes/rewards that are cost-efficient (through scalability and delivery) and immediately deliverable to consumers.
8. Mass media owned and controlled less by big companies and more by individuals.
   Think of how much content is consumer-generated (mySpace, blogs, You-Tube, etc.). More to come.
9. Everything is getting smaller.
   How does this impact your message? There will be less space to use for getting your message across on small phones or PDAs versus TVs or computer monitors.
10. Interactive in more places.
    A wireless world. Interactive will be everywhere: On billboards, in stores, sports arenas, etc. Imagine a frequent shopper card that has RFID (Radio Frequency ID) in it. In-store messages can change for each consumer as they walk through the store.
11. "The Unknown"
    Yes, there will always be something that you can't predict. The key is to be open to seeing the new and different, and be willing to embrace it and experiment with it. Every marketer wants to be the "first," but in actuality the risk of the unknown prevents people from ultimately acting on that statement. There is comfort and security in the present – the known (but there may not be a future in it). The key is recognizing the unknown, or unexpected, and carefully, not recklessly, placing the right bet. Be ready by building experimentation, risk, even failure into your marketing budget. If you only budget against guaranteed, proven marketing models, you will be a follower, not a leader, and perhaps, even a loser.

The moves we see today and the predictions for the future are small in the universe of communications, but they are incredibly significant as a sea change takes place in communications and marketing. A war has begun to stake out territories of influence with today's generation of consumers and, in the end, relevance will win. How that relevance expresses itself and beckons the consumer to lean forward is the key to a marketer's – and a brand's – future success.

The prognosis is clear and direct, as is the message to marketers: Embrace change – respect the consumer and address him on his terms – and succeed, or remain a technological and promotional snail and become a college text case study in failure.

It is that simple. It is that real. Welcome to the Post-Digital Revolution Era, the New World of Marketing.

Printed in the United States
103993LV00003B/226-618/P

9 781598 584288